Where Are We Headed?

Adventism after San Antonio

William G. Johnsson

Where Are We Headed? Copyright © 2017 by William G. Johnsson

For information contact:
Oak and Acorn Publishing
PO Box 5005
Westlake Village, CA 91359-5005

Cover image: Gergen Bakhshetyan/Shutterstock

Cover design by Lindsey Weigley

First Edition: April 2017

10 9 8 7 6 5 4 3 2 1

For

The Undaunted—women in ministry

Contents

About This Book

No tears in the writer, no tears in the reader. No surprise in the writer, no surprise in the reader. —Robert Frost

YOU MIGHT CALL THIS BOOK MY ISAAC. No, I'm not quite up to Abraham's century yet, but the project was conceived and written within my 82nd year.

Isaac was unexpected; so was this book. Usually my mind works on ideas for a book for a long time, often years. But not this one: it came out of the blue, over and done in less than a year.

Put it down to the 2015 General Conference Session in San Antonio. I didn't attend the Session, but I followed it from afar. Some of what I heard and saw affected me profoundly, especially the manner in which the most-awaited item on the agenda—the issue of ordination of women ministers—was handled.

For a couple of weeks after the Session, I moped and grumped around the house and generally made life miserable for my sweet-natured spouse. Then it hit me: Instead of fussing, do what you do best—write about it!

So I did. I worked the issue out of my system. That was that. Done. No plans to take it further.

But, even while I was writing on the women's issue, I kept getting emails and telephone calls about other aspects of the Session. I resisted the thought of going further, but slowly a pattern began to form in my head.

So I tried another topic. The writing came fast, easily. Then another and another....

Recent thinking, speaking, and writing all came together. Almost before I realized it or planned for it, I had a book.

Unexpected. Like Isaac.

The name Isaac means "he laughs." Abraham and Sarah laughed when the angels told them that Sarah would give birth to a son. They laughed in unbelief, at the absurdity of the idea.

But Sarah gave birth. Now there was laughter all around—the laughter of joy, of amazement, of gratitude.

Not quite all around. Abraham already had a son, but not by Sarah. He had grown tired of waiting, taken Hagar to his bed, fathered Ishmael.

Now Isaac was born. Hagar and Ishmael weren't laughing with the rest.

Likewise with my Isaac: I have experienced sharply mixed emotions in writing this manuscript. In a few places what I have to say may give heartburn to some of my former colleagues, whom I still consider friends. So, dear friends, I recommend that you keep a bottle of Tums nearby as you read! Whatever you may think of my ideas, be assured that I wrote what I did only after a lot of consideration and prayer. I promised the Lord and myself that the book would not go forward unless I was clear that its impact would be redemptive.

Several people provided invaluable assistance in this project. First, as ever, my guiding star Noelene: she not only keyed in the manuscript from my handwritten scrawl but also gave wise counsel concerning the content. When once or twice I hesitated, contemplating what publication might cost me personally, she encouraged me to look at the bigger picture—the benefit to hurting pastors and lay people.

Ray Tetz and Brad Newton from the Pacific Union gave enthusiastic support to the project and its publication. I am indebted to them.

Rosy Tetz edited the manuscript; Alberto Valenzuela translated it into Spanish. Many thanks! Muchas gracias!

In several chapters the book draws upon my recent speaking and writing: chapter 3, "The Chosen," on my address to the Adventist Society for Religious Studies' annual meeting in Atlanta, Georgia, of November 21, 2015; chapter 4, "Waiting for Jesus," on my address given at the Charles E. Weniger Award for Excellence, February 21, 2015; chapter 5, "The Message," on my presentation to The One Project in Seattle, February 2016; and chapter 7, "Adventists and Creation," on my article "Christ and Creation," published in the book *In the Beginning: Science and Scripture Confirm Creation*, ed. Bryan W. Ball (Pacific Press, 2012). In chapter 6, "Organization," I quote James Standish's editorial, "Thoughts," published in the *South Pacific Record*, July 2015. I thank Dr. Standish for this material. And in chapter 10, "The Promise of Adventism," I quote from the story told by Dr. Richard Hart, President of Loma Linda University Health, in the June 2016 "Notes from the President."

All royalties from this book will go to a worthy ministry. In the end it's not about me or for me—only Jesus.

Foreword

*Our chief want is someone who will inspire us to be what
we know we could be.*—Ralph Waldo Emerson

s passionate about the health and growth of the Seventh-
day Adventist church in his retirement as he was during
his long career of service, Bill Johnsson contemplated the
life of the church after the summer of 2015 with two questions in
mind: What issues are shaping the Adventist church? How shall we
respond?

Elder William Johnsson served as the editor of the Adventist
Review from 1982 to 2006. For nearly 25 years his observations on
these two questions were the first page that readers turned to on Sabbath afternoons as they picked up the latest copy of the Review.

Since retiring, Johnsson has continued to write and speak.
Prompted by the important issues that came before the church in
2015, in this book Elder Johnsson moves easily and effectively into
the role of pastor and teacher that he knows so well—and that we
have long appreciated.

These questions are deeply personal for Pastor Johnsson. While
the good doctor takes on various relevant topics, his greater interest
is apparent almost immediately: to prompt a discussion about faithfulness and commitment. To better understand what it means to be

a disciple of Christ and a Seventh-day Adventist. To bring the discussion back to our shared mission and purpose.

Oak & Acorn Publishing is a resource publishing enterprise initiated by the Pacific Union Conference of Seventh-day Adventists. It will draw on the talents of academically trained pastors and theologians who reside in the west. Oak & Acorn will allow for the development of resources to serve ministries of varying sizes and will utilize e-publishing technologies for distribution.

As will be typical of future resources, both English and Spanish versions of *Where Are We Headed?* are available, and the books can be ordered as electronic books or as print books through Amazon publishing.

Our prayer is that God will be glorified through this volume and through the work of this new publishing venture. And our hope is that *Where Are We Headed?* will challenge and affirm your life and ministry.

Preface

Tipping Point

If we could just know where we are, and whither we are tending, we could then better judge what to do, and how to do it.—Abraham Lincoln, 1858

SAN ANTONIO WAS A TIPPING POINT in the history of the Seventh-day Adventist Church. The General Conference Session of 2015 exposed and widened fault lines that had been developing for a long time. In later years the Session will be seen as a moment comparable to the 1888 Minneapolis convocation, when two views of the church, two possibilities, met face to face.

The big issue in San Antonio, of course, was the women's ordination question. After passionate debate, the sharply divided vote left the unity of world Adventism in tatters. Many delegates, plus others who were not delegates, came away disillusioned, feeling upset by what they considered manipulation of the process.

Although the "No" side prevailed, its victory came at a heavy price. The events of the fateful day troubled me greatly. When a former General Conference President, someone who served with distinction and who with his spouse gave many years of mission service to the people of Africa, is hissed and booed because he makes a speech in support of women's ordination, I have to ask: *Whatever is going on? Is this my church?* I waited for a public apology from those in leadership. None was forthcoming, at the time or subsequently.

It was, I think, a truly sad day for the Seventh-day Adventist Church. I am ashamed at what transpired.

As major as was the discussion concerning the role of women, that issue was but part of something far larger. Adventism is split down the middle. The split is not merely geographical between the North and the global South—it is more complicated. Like the two babies struggling in Rebekah's womb, two Adventist churches are aborning:

—a church with ordained women clergy struggling with a church that limits the ministry to males;

—a church that engages society with a church that isolates itself from society in a sectarian stance;

—a church that rests confidently in the promise of the Second Coming with a church that stresses the imminence of Jesus' return;

—a church that among all Christians is foremost in uplifting Calvary with a church that wraps the Cross in a package of messages;

—a church that downsizes the upper echelons and focuses on the grass roots with a church increasingly bureaucratic and autocratic;

—a church that exults in the Creator and His creation with a church focused on defending the when of Creation;

—a church that sees its mission as making men and women whole with a church fixated on counting heads;

—a church that adopts a principled interpretation of Scripture with a church that comes to the Word in a flat, literalistic manner;

—a church for whom Ellen White's writings are inspired counsel but subject to the authority of Scripture with a church that raises them to a level of equality with Scripture, or above.

I have deliberately sharpened the alternatives. The position for many Adventists lies between the two poles. Overall, however, the point holds true: two radically different versions of Adventism are competing for the future. Which one will prevail? Where are we headed?

The Seventh-day Adventist Church will survive. It will not merely survive; it will grow—but not uniformly. In some regions of the world where it has been in existence for more than a century, it is on life support; it may fade away. Elsewhere it will advance from strength to strength. World membership by official count is approaching 20 million; that figure will be reached and far outstripped.

I make the above assertions confidently because I believe that, more than any human factor, the Risen Lord is Head of the Church. He is Lord of the invisible church scattered among its many different communions in all the world—Adventists can claim no exclusive status—but I believe that Jesus has brought the Adventist movement into being to proclaim an end-time message.

There is a specialness about the Adventist church, a specialness that our "remnant" teaching attempts to articulate, even though we express that idea in terms that are easily misunderstood.

I love this church and have given most of my life in an attempt to build it up. This little book, although it may include some sharp points, comes out of a heart of love. If I have a quarrel with aspects of what is happening—and I do—it is a lover's quarrel. I will not benefit financially from this work; I am donating all royalties.

I also believe this: the Lord will not save us from ourselves. The

Lord doesn't prevent us from making foolish choices, just as He didn't spare the church of old, Israel, from itself. Thus, although Adventism will continue to advance, while the numbers will roll on, what sort of church will we be?

I am not a historian, but what I read of the development of the early Christian church leads me to profound heart-searching. In the second century the church departed from Jesus' teachings and practice. It moved from a fellowship where clergy and laity weren't separated by a sharp line—because all believers constituted the *laos*, the people of God—to one that was more and more dominated by the clergy. From a church built on Jesus the Servant-Leader, who came not to be served but to serve (Mark 10:45), to one that increasingly claimed and exercised ecclesiastical authority. From a church based on Scripture alone to one that mingled the Bible with traditions and ecclesiastical pronouncements.

We Adventists are now in our second century. As I compare the church of the second century AD with the Adventist church in its second century, what I find scares me. Leaders of our church should honestly undertake such a study, unwelcome though it may be.

In the remaining chapters of this work I shall take up in turn ten areas where Adventism is divided. With each I will point to what I believe the Scriptures teach. With this book I hope to call Adventists, "the people of the Book," back to the Book.

For many years, as editor of the *Adventist Review* and *Adventist World*, I endeavored to share the truth with the people, even when the truth hurt. We Adventists aren't good at this. We like to hear "a good report." We'd rather hear about the large number of people baptized during an evangelistic campaign than learn how many of them were no longer attending church a year later. We are big on appearances, ultra careful to look right and sound right, seemingly more concerned about how others regard us than does the Lord, who reads hearts.

Some readers, especially my former colleagues, may be surprised at the content of this book. Be assured, dear brothers and sisters, that I am not judging you. And I freely admit it: I may be wrong. However, the times demand that I tell it as I see it, and tell it without beating around the bush.

CHAPTER ONE

Women's Ordination: The Battle is Over

So God created man in his own image, in the image of God created he him; male and female created he them.—Genesis 1:27

THE ROLE OF WOMEN MINISTERS in the Seventh-day Adventist Church has been debated almost from our beginnings as a denomination in 1863. This was because in the pioneer period women served in ministerial roles. More than that, one woman in particular played a huge role both in our development and in public proclamation. That woman was Ellen G. White, rightly regarded as one of the founders of the movement. In addition to her counsels and writing, she preached extensively and with authority, not only counseling General Conference presidents but on occasion rebuking them.

Not all the early Adventists were comfortable with women occupying the pulpit. We know this because leaders like Uriah Smith took up the matter in the *Review and Herald*, addressing objections based on 1 Corinthians 14:34: "Women should remain silent in the churches. They are not allowed to speak, but must be in submission, as the Law says."

In 1881, only 18 years after the Seventh-day Adventist Church officially organized, the General Conference Session took up a surprising item—a resolution that women who had demonstrated the qualities of a minister might be ordained to the gospel ministry:

> Resolved, that females possessing the necessary qualifications to fill that position, may, with perfect propriety be set apart by ordination to the work of the ministry.

After discussion, the matter was referred to the General Conference Committee for consideration and was never heard from again. (The GC Committee at that time consisted of three men.)

Ellen White's position on this item can be debated. She remained silent, at the time and subsequently. Her silence can be interpreted as either in favor of or opposed to the ordination of women ministers; no conclusive argument can be advanced. What we may be sure of, however, is that if the Lord had given her light on the matter, she would have shared it. Clearly, she did not receive divine counsel on this item, which a century later would develop into a hot-button issue among Adventists.

She herself was never ordained by the laying on of hands. Nevertheless, she carried the official credentials of an ordained minister throughout her long life of service. The credentials issued to her at times had the word "ordained" crossed out, but mostly they did not.

God had called Ellen; she had a divine anointing. Any laying on by human hands could not have added to what the Holy Spirit already had made obvious.

Ellen passed to her rest, full of years, in 1915. After her death the number of women in ministry slowly declined. The church forgot that once it had given a prominent place to women, with several serving at various times as Treasurer of the General Conference.

With the rise of the women's movement in American society, Adventists again began to encourage women in ministry. Under the leadership of Neal C. Wilson, who was then president of the North American Division, churches were encouraged to appoint and ordain women elders. Then Seminary doors opened for women who felt called to pastoral ministry as the division provided scholarships for their study. By the early 1980s women were serving in ministry as "ministers in pastoral care," employed and, after ordination as local elders, authorized to carry out almost all the duties of ordained ministers—preaching, presiding at the Communion service, and officiating in weddings and funerals. (The only exception was organizing new churches, a duty that comes to most Adventist clergy rarely, if at all.)

The course of events—women elders, scholarships for ministerial preparation, associates in pastoral care—put women on the path toward ordination. But then a new element was added to the process. All the actions up to this point encouraging women to enter the ministry had been taken by vote of the Annual Council, not a General Conference Session. In the 1980s Elder Wilson, now General Conference President, became convinced that authorization for women as ordained pastors required a vote representing the world church, that is, a General Conference Session. The chief reason advanced was that we are a world church and ordination to ministry confers authority for ministers to serve anywhere in the world field.

The General Conference under Wilson's direction appointed a commission to consider the matter, with instructions to present a recommendation to the 1990 General Conference Session. I was deeply involved in the work of this commission, not only reporting on its progress but also contributing to its discussions.

The commission had many members, and it soon became obvious that a consensus would not be reached. The problem was that no clear direction from inspired writings—either from the Bible or the Ellen White corpus—could be established. The commission therefore recommended that the Seventh-day Adventist Church not proceed with ordination of women ministers at that time. This recommendation, after lengthy discussion, was voted by the General Conference Session, which met in Indianapolis.

That same General Conference Session also took a related action, however. It authorized women to serve as associates in pastoral care, performing the same ministerial functions that the earlier Annual Council actions had stipulated.

But the debate wasn't over. Five years later, in 1995, the women's issue again featured prominently at the General Conference Session, meeting in Utrecht, The Netherlands. This time the body took up a request from the North American Division that it be authorized to move ahead with women's ordination. After debate marked by passion and heat, the North American Division request suffered a sound defeat.

Inevitably the issue would reappear. The number of women ministers in North America continued to increase, and some other divisions also began to appoint women to pastoral positions. When Elder Ted Wilson, son of the former General Conference President, was elected in 2010 to the same office, he announced that a commission would be set up to study the question of ordination itself as well as women's ordination, with the 2015 Session once again to take up the matter.

I will pass quickly over subsequent developments since they are still fresh in memory. The commission was appointed—it was large, with some 100 members—and took up first the question of ordination itself, then women's ordination. On the first question, a broad consensus formed that in Adventist understanding ordination does not confer any special status or gifts on the person being ordained. (Here the commission could look to specific statements of Ellen White.) On the issue of women's ordination, however, a sharp division within the commission became evident. Nevertheless, a clear majority favored ordination of women ministers, without ordination being forced on the church in regions where it was not accepted.

So to San Antonio. I was not a delegate to the 2015 General Conference Session, nor did I attend. I followed by television the proceedings of July 8, when the full day was to have been devoted to discussion of the issue. And later I heard from delegates and others who attended.

From all I saw and heard, I conclude that it was a sorry day in Adventist history. The meeting developed into a circus, with delegates raising numerous points of order and taking the time from the discussion that had been promised. Saddest of all was the shameful reaction to the remarks of past General Conference President Jan Paulsen.

After the Session, some women pastors went through a difficult period. They were confronted by members who demanded they quit because the General Conference Session had voted that women should not serve in the Adventist ministry. It did nothing of the sort: the issue debated was whether each division might be free to ordain women ministers if they considered such a course helpful to advance mission. (The issue corresponded to the one debated in 1995 in Utrecht.)

Already, in the years leading up to San Antonio, some unions had ordained women pastors without General Conference authorization. Some administrators after the Session vote began to question whether these "rebellious" entities of the church should be subject to some form of discipline. Eventually, however, that line of thinking did not prevail among leaders—wisely, I think, for reasons that will become apparent below.

So, are we back to square one on women's ordination? Will the issue continue to use up time, effort, and money for the foreseeable future, or did San Antonio put it behind us?

What Lies Ahead?

I will tell you what lies ahead. The war is over—San Antonio settled it, but not in the manner some Adventists would like to think. The war is over because the ordination of women pastors will spread rapidly throughout most parts of the world church.

In quite a short time—maybe five years, certainly less than ten years, we'll wonder: What was that all about? Why did we waste so much time and money that could have been used far more profitably on mission?

That's what lies ahead. I am certain of it. Here are my reasons:

1. **The wall is toppling.** The horse is out of the barn; it cannot be corralled; it's gone. By the end of 2015, one could count at least a

dozen union conferences that had broken in one way or another with official General Conference policy in this matter. Hardly a month passes but another joins them. This is a movement. The snowball is rolling; it cannot be stopped.

What do I mean? In North America, where women first were ordained, new ordinations have gone forward. Conferences have voted to open all administrative offices to women; by policy conference or union presidential office requires ordination. In several areas male pastors have exchanged their credentials as ordained ministers to the same as those issued to women pastors—"commissioned" instead of "ordained."

Outside North America several unions have taken actions that all ministers, whether male or female, will henceforth carry identical credentials—or they have issued statements announcing that, after thorough consideration of both the findings of the commission on ordination and the action voted in San Antonio, they have voted to proceed with the ordination of women.

Two of these actions are especially noteworthy because they come, not from North America or Europe, but from areas often regarded as opposing women in ministry. In both South Africa and Papua New Guinea a woman pastor has been officially commissioned into pastoral ministry.

From a biblical standpoint, ordination and commissioning are the same. In the New Testament we find only commissioning; "ordination" as a term does not exist. (The reference to Jesus' ordaining the Twelve in Mark 3:14 is found only in the King James Version. The Greek word that is used indicates choosing or appointing, as the New King James Version and all modern translations attest.)

Unfortunately, most Adventists probably are unaware of these developments. The official church press has not made them known; one has to turn to independent Adventist sources. And that itself, I believe, is something that is untrue to our heritage.

2. A moral issue. That's why it isn't going away. Three General Conference Sessions, three "thumbs down" votes, but it isn't going away.

A moral issue means conscience. Conscience, as Martin Luther observed before the Diet of Worms: "Here I stand; I can do no other." Conscience, as in Ellen White's classic: "The greatest want of the world is the want of men . . . men whose conscience is as true to duty as the needle to the pole" (*Education*, p. 57).

Nine professors from the Seventh-day Adventist Theological Seminary at Berrien Springs, Michigan, sent individual letters to the General Conference following the negative vote in San Antonio. Each professor, male, requested that his ministerial credentials be changed so that he would no longer be classified as an ordained minister. These professors wrote to the General Conference because the Seminary is a General Conference institution; their employer is the General Conference, so their credentials originate there.

I can only imagine the consternation these letters must have caused to the good brethren at headquarters. A request to have one's ordination credentials changed—unheard of! No provision for it is found in the policy.

Why did these nine men, who exposed themselves to some risk by their course of action, send the letters? Conscience. They see the women's question as a moral issue that overrides ecclesiastical votes.

For many years I was in the thick of the theological debates over women's ordination. I heard a lot of theological argumentation, and much theological hair-splitting. In all these discussions of theology I heard almost nothing about the ethical concerns involved.

The Lord, however, calls us to be people of deep moral sensibility. He is less concerned about our getting every jot and tittle of theology correct than He is about how we relate to moral issues. He tells us that what He expects of us is "to act justly and to love mercy and to walk humbly with your God" (Micah 6:8, NIV). Jesus echoed this passage as He condemned the teachers of the law and the Pharisees. "You have neglected the more important matters of the law—justice, mercy and faithfulness," He said (Matthew 23:23, NIV).

Let me share a concrete example to show that women's ordination is a moral issue. When I taught at the Seminary, among the students in my classes were a husband and wife, both of whom felt called to ministry. Both were good students, she a little better than he. Both graduated with Master of Divinity degrees. Both found employment as pastors in the same conference, but of different churches. Both served capably as shepherds of their respective congregations.

But there the parallels ceased. After several years he was ordained; she was not, because the Seventh-day Adventist church does not ordain women.

Is this not unjust? Is this not discriminatory treatment? How does it measure up with what the Lord requires, as stated in Micah 6:8 and Matthew 23:23?

3. Bogus arguments. Many of those Adventists who oppose the ordination of women have employed arguments that, on investigation, are falsified. Even though these arguments were put forward out of sincere motives, that does not make them correct.

An argument that I heard frequently in the past, not as often in recent years, is that the push for women's ordination springs from the "women's lib" movement. Those who regarded the movement negatively then attributed to Adventist women pastors the stereotype of aggressive, militant, angry individuals.

That line of reasoning, however, is patently bogus. Discussion of women's ordination among Adventists predated the "women's lib" movement by 70 or more years: we already noted that the 1881 General Conference Session considered a resolution favoring ordaining qualified women pastors. Furthermore, the current push among us comes not from women but from men, especially ordained ministers in several different countries who have surrendered their credentials in solidarity with their female counterparts.

In recent debates, the ordination of women has been linked to ordination of gays. The claim is made that the history of other denominations that have ordained women clergy shows that the next step inevitably follows—ordination of homosexuals.

Once again the argument falls flat in view of the facts. From its beginning, a church that arose shortly after us placed women alongside men in total equality in ministry. I refer to The Salvation Army. From its outset women have not only served in ministry but have been elected to its highest posts, including the supreme one of General.

No one today could identify The Salvation Army, widely respected for its humanitarian activities, as being a church with gay clergy. So the argument about inevitability—first ordain women, then ordain gays—is bogus.

Another argument against women clergy reasons that this position is against the natural order. From the Creation, God put in place the ordering of society, giving males authority over women. Therefore, to permit a woman to preach and lead males in a congregation violates the order established by the Lord.

In recent years this line of approach has been developed into an elaborate "headship" theology that involves relations in heaven as well as on earth. In this schema God is the head of Christ and man is the head of woman. This is the way it is in heaven and the way it is supposed to be on earth.

As convincing as the argument may appear on casual examination, it is flawed. In the beginning—at the Creation—God made male and female in His image (Genesis 1:26-27). They were complementary, not in subordinate relationship. And to suggest that the Son is eternally subordinate to the Father lowers the Son's status as One who is eternally God—God in all respects—and runs close to an ancient heresy.

For followers of Jesus Christ, He is the last word in doctrine and practice. In His teachings, Jesus sharply rebuked ideas of headship: "Jesus called them together and said, 'You know that the rulers of the Gentiles lord it over them, and their high officials exercise authority over them. Not so with you. Instead, whoever wants to become great among you must be your servant, and whoever wants to be first must be your slave—just as the Son of Man did not come to be served, but to serve, and to give his life as a ransom for many'" (Matthew 20:25-28, NIV).

Jesus set the example in self-denial:

Who, being in very nature God,
    did not consider equality with God something
to be used to his own advantage;
rather, he made himself nothing
    by taking the very nature of a servant,
    being made in human likeness.

> And being found in appearance as a man,
>> he humbled himself
>> by becoming obedient to death—
>>> even death on a cross! (Philippians 2:6-8, NIV).

Thus, the arguments against women's ordination drawn from history or the Bible are bogus, no matter how sincerely addressed. And their failure has become evident to an ever-widening circle of Seventh-day Adventists.

4. Millennials. They not only support women's ordination, they find the church's official position out of touch and baffling. Their generation has grown up with settled convictions concerning equality. To find their church still unable to adopt women's ordination jars with their sensibilities about justice and equality. The Seventh-day Adventist Church—their church—lags behind society in moral values, instead of leading the way.

Thirty years ago, when the church in North America intensely debated the woman's issue, our two children were in college. They and their friends followed the arguments pro and con and the official developments with great interest. On one occasion several of our son's friends were in the Washington area and came to our house for a meal. At that time I was in the thick of the debate, serving on the commissions that were set up in turn to study the matter. Terry's friends, all bright young students, expressed puzzlement that the church was even studying the question. What is there to study? They wanted to know. To them the answer was self-evident, in need of no further study.

Back then, the Seventh-day Adventist Church turned away from a clear vote for women's ordination. Terry and his friends were disappointed and disillusioned. Their reaction was typical of many others of their generation. The image of the church suffered a severe setback in the minds of these idealistic youth. Many who once entertained ideas of joining the work force to advance the church's mission had second thoughts. Over time, large numbers drifted away altogether from association with the church.

Only the Lord knows how great were the losses we sustained over this issue.

Today, we face a similar crisis—similar, but even worse. The debate in San Antonio with its negative vote brought huge and widespread disappointment. Not to have an action from the world church in assembly supporting women's ordination was bad enough, but to have the General Conference Session vote down permission for each division to decide the matter on what was best for its mission seemed incredible, incomprehensible.

Our church has come to a critical moment in her history. We face the prospect of large numbers of our best and brightest giving up on the church and just walking away. Some have made it clear that they intend to stay and fight; many others, sadly, have had enough of what they have concluded is an organization hopelessly blind to moral concerns.

The present situation is intolerable. Women's ordination will come and must come. Tragically, it will come out of the pain of seeing young men and women leaving the church.

5. Laughter. In any battle laughter is a powerful weapon. When people can laugh in a difficult situation, they are already a good way along toward winning. Laughter shows that they have taken the long view and know that, although the immediate scene is dark, the end will be bright.

Sometimes a situation becomes absurd, so contrary to reality that the best thing to do is to laugh at it. Today in North America and beyond, millennial Adventists are laughing at Church leaders. They laugh, not out of disrespect, but out of the sheer absurdity of the church's official stance on women's ordination:

—a church with a woman as one of its founders?

—a church that opened its doors to women far ahead of the times, admitting them to the newly opened medical school in Loma Linda?

—a church where a woman can serve as university president?

—a church where women can preach, baptize, officiate at weddings and funerals, preside at the Lord's Supper?

—a church that already has ordained women in leadership in China?

—all these in a church that denies women one piece of the pie: ordination to the ministry?

We Adventist have put ourselves in a logical and theological bind. The official practice doesn't make sense, and the young people see it. Laughter is the only recourse—other than shaking their heads and walking away.

Millennials have their own system of communication. It bypasses the long-established print network on which church leaders have relied to get their message out. The new method, totally outside official oversight, has taken over: social media. This is how millennials communicate today; this is how they get the news.

Here's a statistic from San Antonio: on Wednesday, July 8, the day of the debate on women's ordination, more than three million people went on the Spectrum Twitter site. Three million! I find that staggering. Granted that some may have visited the site more than once, the number is still huge.

Note: this was the Spectrum site, not an official one. Millennials were interested; they got involved. And they were unhappy about the day, and especially the negative vote.

In this age of Twitter and Facebook, new Adventist websites have sprung up. They cover the waterfront—from critical to serious to funny. One, anonymous, pokes gentle fun at what is viewed as Adventist absurdities. Many of the postings are sophomoric, but occasionally they're hilarious. When Pope Francis visited Washington, DC, the website ran a satirical piece that described how he made a surprise visit to General Conference headquarters in Silver Spring, MD. He drove up in his Fiat pope-mobile to personally thank church leaders for holding the line on ordination!

Unsolicited Advice to My Brethren

For many years I was one of "the brethren" at church headquarters. Once I had voice and vote; now I have voice and pen. And this is what I share with my brothers and sisters called to leadership: The war is over. Don't try to patch up the wall to keep women out. Already it's cracking wide open. It's bound to topple.

Listen, the young people are laughing. And leaving.

Look around, women are in ministry all over, and the Lord is blessing their efforts.

The time has come. In fact, it's long overdue.

A wave of women's ordinations is sweeping over the Adventist world.

The dawn is breaking. Don't try to hold it back.

God's truth is marching on.

CHAPTER TWO

The Chosen:
Exclusive or Inclusive?

He drew a circle that shut me out—
Heretic, rebel, a thing to flout.
But love and I had the wit to win:
We drew a circle that took him in.
—Edwin Markham

NOT LONG AFTER THE CLOSE of the San Antonio General Conference Session, I received a long letter from a pastor who had been selected to be a delegate. I know well the qualities of good mind, love of the Lord, and love of the Seventh-day Adventist Church this person brings to ministry.

Let me quote extensively from the letter. You may find it disturbing; I do. You may be tempted to dismiss these thoughts as coming from someone with a chip on their shoulder, a malcontent. But you would be wrong. This pastor, who belongs to a generation much younger than mine, is an excellent minister, valued by conference administrators.

Early on the letter mentions the women's ordination issue. Like many others at the Session, this pastor was troubled about the way the issue was presented as well as the final vote. But that wasn't all—not by a long shot.

"The issue of ordination, however, was nowhere near as disturbing as the greater picture of the church as a whole that I saw. Arrogant. Exclusive. Cultish. Fixated on end-time events. Willing to be led by popular celebrities. Disrespectful of theologians. And unwilling to see God at work anywhere else in the world but through us. Fear, pride, and control were at the helm rather than Jesus.

"As I have processed it since, I feel one of our most significant issues is our false idea of remnant. A belief that our denomination is exclusively God's remnant, rather than the more biblical picture (at least from my perspective) of God having a remnant people on the earth, as he always has, as us being given added light to share in this period of earth's history.

"But the issue that I see this remnant theology being for us today, is the arrogance that it has given us as a denomination—the belief that all other churches are of the devil, deceived, dangerous; the fear of reading outside of our own denomination, of working with other churches, of learning from them. This theology has built huge walls between us and the rest of Christianity. And we spend far too much time and energy trying to preserve ourselves, to stay distinct.

"And then there is the pressure that it puts on us: we have to be always right, because we are God's remnant. In other words, because we are God's remnant, everything that has gone before must not be questioned because if we do question it, we are questioning our very identity. No reviewing of past theology, no questioning, no room for further light because the idea of truly questioning anything challenges our ideas of being the remnant. Of course we would not admit this—we are all about present truth, but that is not what I see in our very deep-seated culture.

"We are like Israel of old, fixated on our own kingdom, not seeing Jesus walking through our temples and cities. And when He does speak through people, we find them threatening. They threaten our structure, our tradition, our identity, our public evangelism budgets, and so we silence them—usually by suggesting that they are heretics or Jesuits."

The letter concluded: "Having said all that, God is still on His throne. I am His child, and there are incredible people he has brought into our lives to journey with, and so there is much to be joyful about. And though the worldwide church in its present state has very little that I identify with, I know in my heart that this is where God has me, and so I will continue to serve."

Is this pastor a lone voice in the wilderness? Not at all. I am convinced that the sentiments of the letter are shared by large numbers of others, especially in America, Europe, and the South Pacific.

I urge leaders of the church to weigh carefully what I have shared. It is painful, but it is reality.

What sort of Adventist Church will the future reveal? An exclusive body, so sure that it is right and everyone else is wrong that it feels we can "go it alone," shunning contact and cooperation with others? Or will it take a broader view, realizing that, while God has raised us up and given us a message for the world, He is a BIG God, far bigger than our small sphere, and that He is working out His plan through many different agencies?

Interestingly, the official stance of our church toward other Christians is inclusive, not exclusive. As far back as 1870 we find the following action voted by the Eighth Annual Session of the General Conference:

> RESOLVED, that for the sake of our blessed Redeemer we desire to cultivate fraternal feelings, and maintain friendly relations, with all who name the name of Christ; and in particular with those who in common with us hold to the unpopular doctrine of the second advent of our Savior near.

For about 100 years Adventist relations with other churches have been officially defined and guided by a policy in the *General Conference Working Policy*, O 110, "Relationship With Other Christian Churches and Religious Organizations." In part it states: "We recognize those agencies that lift up Christ before men as a part of the divine plan for evangelization of the world, and we hold in high esteem Christian men and women in other communions who are engaged in winning souls to Christ."

Unfortunately, as in some other areas, our official stand is not matched by our practice. Many Adventists, both lay and leaders, are wary of contact with others who aren't one of "us."

We need to go back to the Bible for direction—right back to Jesus, our Lord and Savior.

The Town or the Desert?

Two young men began to preach—so similar, so different.

They were related and about the same age. Both had been born in unusual circumstances. They gave the same God-given message: "Repent! For the kingdom of heaven is at hand!" Both attracted large crowds and a band of followers. Both died young, cut down in ghastly executions, denied justice.

Therein the similarities end. One, the older, grew up in the desert; the other in a small town, but with a city only a few miles away. One dressed like an old-time prophet, in leather and camel hair; the other in the tunic (*chiton*) and coat that ordinary people wore. One ate food that he found in the desert—locusts and wild honey; the other the bread and fish that constituted the local diet. One preached that God's kingdom was imminent; the other that the kingdom already was breaking in. One proclaimed that the Messiah was about to appear; the other declared Himself to be that long-promised Anointed One.

One carried on his ministry in the desert he was familiar with. He preached and the people came to him: "In those days John the Baptist came, preaching in the wilderness of Judea" (Matthew 3:1, NIV). The other, however, went to the people, where they were. He was a Man of the public square. For the first preacher, ministry focused in words— he preached. But Jesus ministered to the whole person—teaching, preaching, healing, making people whole. "Jesus went throughout Galilee, teaching in their synagogues, proclaiming the good news of the kingdom, and healing every disease and sickness among the people" (Matthew 4:23, NIV).

John the Baptist was God's person for the times. He was, as the Gospel of John tells us, a man who was sent from God (John 1:6). Jesus commended him in the highest terms: "Truly I tell you, among those born of women there has not risen anyone greater than John the Baptist" (Matthew 11:11, NIV).

We Seventh-day Adventists take special interest in John the Baptist. In important respects he was the forerunner of the Messiah, called to announce His imminent appearing—like us. For some Adventists the attraction extends further: to John's simplicity of dress and his strict diet. (Although, with all the food fads among us, I have yet to find the "locusts and wild honey way to better health!")

Over the years, Adventists have tended to follow John's approach to ministry rather than Jesus'. We have been a people of the country, spurning the city, proclaiming the message and calling the people to come to us. In general we have avoided the public square, have looked upon it with suspicion. We built our schools and hospitals "far from the madding crowd." It used to be said that at the end of every bad road you could find an Adventist hospital.

The times, of course, are a-changin'. Cities have grown up around our colleges and health centers. Population has aggregated in cities. And "the world" has invaded even the remotest corners of our desert—through the Internet, cell phones, and television.

All along, some among us lived and served in the public square. African American Adventists were, and are, largely city people. And our hospitals, carrying on a massive ministry, have placed Adventists solidly in the public square—and thereby, I think, have helped to save us from some of the extremes that often accompany apocalyptic movements.

It's high time for Adventists to move out from the desert and into the public square. It's high time to follow Jesus' method of ministry rather than John's. It's time to leave the comfort zone of the desert.

For a church that likes to boast about having "the truth," it's surprising that we often seem hesitant about taking it beyond our comfort zone. We have a message, and it's good news! The world needs it; the world waits to hear it.

We have let petty, stupid things get in the way of entering the public square. Things like our vegetarian diet. Even the name: Seventh-day Adventist! Will people think we're weird, some kind of cult?

All such reserve is nonsense. The world no longer regards a vegetarian diet as oddball—rather, it's a trendy thing. "Seventh-day Adventists? Who are you and what do you believe? What makes you different from other Christians?" Those are the reactions to our name in these days, when denominational designations and differences count for less and less.

Out of the Comfort Zone

Let me briefly share some of my experiences when I left the Adventist comfort zone for the public square. I will limit myself to just a few of the many from my involvement in interchurch and interfaith activities.

My first experience with interchurch dialogue occurred some 30 years ago. The circumstances were unusual: a group of Evangelical leaders, led by Kenneth Kantzer, then editor of *Christianity Today*, requested a conversation with the Seventh-day Adventist Church. They wished to determine how they should relate to Adventists: could they extend fellowship to us as genuine Christian brothers and sisters, or were we beyond the pale?

At that time relations between Evangelicals and Adventists were mixed. Many Evangelicals regarded us with suspicion; they were openly hostile in their writing and preaching. Some, however, had come into contact with Adventists on a personal basis and had found us to be sincere followers of Christ. On the Adventist side, many among us harbored similarly negative feelings toward the Evangelicals, seeing them, along with other churches in general, as part of Babylon. Because of the mutual distrust, it was agreed from the outset that the discussions would not be made public by either side.

We met for a few days at GC headquarters in Takoma Park, MD. The Evangelicals brought a couple of leading biblical scholars, with Kenneth Kantzer heading up the group. The Adventist side consisted of Gerhard Hasel, Bert Beach, Bill Shea, and me.

The meeting was not a true dialogue, inasmuch as all the questions were directed toward the Adventists. The Fundamental Beliefs formed the focus, with two in particular soon singled out for close examination. They were—as you might have guessed—the statements on Ellen White and the Ministry of Christ in the Heavenly Sanctuary.

Relations during the days together were cordial but guarded. The Evangelical leaders raised polite but penetrating questions. They queried us in depth until they were satisfied that they understood our position with regard to the Bible—do we truly look to the Scriptures as the foundation of our teaching? And regarding the gospel—does our Sanctuary doctrine diminish the all-sufficient, once-for-all sacrifice of Jesus on Calvary?

After a couple of days of probing, the Evangelicals spent some time together weighing what they had heard. Then they reported back the results of the deliberations: they found nothing in our fundamental beliefs that stood in the way of extending fellowship to Adventists. And well do I remember a statement of Kenneth Kantzer during that final meeting: "Never give up your Sabbath! We Evangelicals are weak in the area of obedience; we need to learn from you!"

How I wished that I could have told our people about this meeting through the pages of the *Review*!

During the 30 years since, relations with Evangelicals have changed dramatically. I have to conclude that those meetings at the General Conference when we sat down with Kenneth Kantzer and his group played a significant role in leading to a new day.

Of the many interchurch dialogues in which I was involved—first as a member of the Adventist team, later as its chair—two stand out because of their impact: the conversation with the Lutherans and the later one with the World Evangelical Alliance.

The first of these involved the Lutheran World Federation, based in Geneva, Switzerland, and representing some 60 Lutheran bodies. We met four times for about one week each during 1994-1998. The exchanges were marked by careful preparation and serious scholarly papers; the scholars came from many different countries.

The initial encounter, which Adventists hosted, convened at Marienhohe Seminaire in Germany. For the first couple of days, the atmosphere was icy. Several from the Lutheran delegation could not conceal their disdain for their Adventist counterparts, whom they viewed as ignorant sectarians.

But as the week progressed a distinct change became obvious. The Lutherans were astonished at our expressions of high esteem for Martin Luther; at first they thought we were not sincere, but eventually they began to see otherwise. At the same time their eyes were opened to the level of scholarly research and integrity that the Adventists exhibited. Among our representatives was Dr. Hans Heinz, who quoted verbatim from Luther's works—in German!

By the close of the week it had become clear to all that a fruitful conversation would be possible and should be pursued. At our invitation, most of the Lutherans altered their travel plans in order to attend Sabbath services. They sat in Sabbath school classes and then heard a gospel-centered sermon. They remarked that the message could have come from a Lutheran pulpit.

During the succeeding years, papers on both sides focused in turn on Justification and Scripture, on Church and Sacraments, and finally, on Eschatology.

By mutual agreement, we left the final round of conversations for the area where we figured the two sides had least in common. The Lutheran papers presented on Eschatology were very thin. By contrast, those from the Adventists let it all hang out, including topics like the Remnant and the Mark of the Beast. Some of the Lutherans almost choked on the Mark of the Beast, and I wondered if the dialogue would break up. After some lively exchanges—to put it mildly—the goodwill built up during the previous three years of conversation brought us all through to a mutually respectful conclusion.

During the final meeting we developed a long statement. It described the nature and progress of our years together and concluded with a series of recommendations to our respective bodies. I quote from the first of these recommendations:

"We recommend that Adventists and Lutherans mutually recognize the basic Christian commitment of the other's faith communion. We recommend that Lutherans in their national and regional church contexts do not treat the Seventh-day Adventist Church as a sect but as a free church and a Christian world communion."

The papers from the dialogue, along with the report, were gathered together and jointly published by the Lutheran World Federation and the General Conference of Seventh-day Adventists. This book, *Lutherans and Adventists in Conversation, 1994-1998*, still circulates in Europe and America.

Most of the dialogues in which I was involved proceeded relatively calmly. However, when we met with representatives from the World Evangelical Alliance, the gloves came off! It quickly became obvious that some of those from the WEA harbored strong suspicions concerning Adventists and were not about to extend fellowship to us.

The first round was held at a Baptist seminary in Prague, the Czech Republic, with the Evangelicals hosting the event. One of their delegates, a pastor from Switzerland, brought two large folders of material that he placed prominently on the table in front of him. He remained silent for the first few days but at length launched into a vitriolic attack based on the contents of the folders. It then became apparent that he had gathered a long list of charges that he had found on the Internet from the writings of former Adventists.

The second and final round, which Adventists hosted, met on the campus of Andrews University. I had strong doubts that it would be possible to arrive at a consensus statement for release to the public. My concerns increased when the Evangelical representatives brought out their draft of the proposed final statement. It was totally unacceptable to us. It stated that Adventists base their distinctive teachings, including the Sabbath, on the writings of Ellen White rather than on the Bible. We protested strongly. At length they invited us to draft an alternative statement.

Bert Beach went to work and produced a succinct piece that squarely laid out areas where both sides agreed and where they disagreed; further, it listed areas of possible cooperation. After a lot of back-and-forthing, and several amendments, the statement was adopted.

Since that encounter, I have noticed a marked change in the way Evangelicals relate to Adventists. In the past when they learned that I was Seventh-day Adventist, a noticeable chill entered the room. Now

I am greeted warmly as a Christian brother. The WEA in its frequent press releases emphasizes that the Seventh-day Adventist Church, while not a member of its body, is in fellowship with its members, who number more than 600 million worldwide.

In my judgment the various official conversations into which we entered—with the Reformed, the Salvation Army, the Mennonites, the Presbyterians, and others—accomplished much good. They helped to correct misunderstandings, to break down stereotypes, to remove prejudice. They benefited me personally: by leaving my Adventist comfort zone, my thinking was broadened and enriched. I met men and women who were not only fine scholars but also devout Christians. And seeing my Adventist beliefs against the canvas of other faith traditions brought new clarity and appreciation. I learned that we need not be hesitant or defensive.

Some of the saints have raised questions about these conversations. They figure that the very process of dialogue entails a compromise of our beliefs. I can tell you that they are wrong and massively wrong. I put to you this question: if Christians from a different church are willing to sit down with us in order to find out what makes us "tick," as it were; if, as some did, they approach us and request us to meet with them, why would we not enter into dialogue wholeheartedly?

I did not see it coming, but the Lord had more in store for me. He would take me far, far out of my comfort zone, beyond all that had gone before. I would meet and dialogue with leaders of Islam.

This is how it happened. As I was about to retire from the *Adventist Review*, my boss, Dr. Jan Paulsen, dangled a surprising invitation before me: Would I continue at the General Conference working part-time as his special assistant to care not only for the interchurch dialogues but to move into the interfaith field? With our church grow-ing rapidly throughout the world, Adventists now had neighbors who were Buddhists, Hindus, Muslims, and so on. My new assignment would involve making contact with leaders of world religions at the highest level possible, seeking to acquaint them with who we are, our values and beliefs.

This task, for which there was no job description and no road map, became my focus during the next eight years. It took me to the Hashemite Kingdom of Jordan numerous times, where I met religious and political leaders who ranged from the chief justice of the nation to Princess Basma, sister of the late King Hussein. Some of these of-ficials became good friends—like Professor Hamdi Morad, imam to the King; Ambassador Hussein abu-Nieman, Jordan's representative to the United Nations; and Judge Amjad B. Shmoot, founder and di-rector of the Arab Bridge Center for Human Rights.

These encounters transformed my perspective, especially con-cerning Islam. I was surprised to learn how approachable these high-level officials are, how little they know about Seventh-day Adventists, how they share belief in the return of Isa (Jesus), and how eager they are to distance themselves from the violent element within Islam.

These contacts eventually yielded a significant result. Under the auspices of the Arab Bridge Center and the International Religious Liberty Association, we convened an all-day symposium at a univer-sity in Amman that addressed the topic "Teaching Respect for Reli-gion." It featured both Adventist and Muslim speakers and attracted dignitaries in Amman; it received major press coverage. The meeting opened with a greeting from the Minister for Religious Affairs.

"Teaching respect for religion"—we badly need that message in the United States today!

My efforts in interfaith relations brought a mixed reaction from Adventists. After several years I wrote an article summarizing my experiences with Muslims; it was published in Adventist World, from where it went viral. Over the years I have received many letters, but this article brought a flood. As the article circulated via the Internet, I continued to hear from the saints for several years. Many of those who wrote were positive. Some were puzzled. And some, blazing hot!

There is a great deal more that I could share about my experiences in interchurch and interfaith relations, but let us turn to the Scriptures.

The Word of the Lord

That word comes from the Book of Hebrews, so loved and so important to Adventists:

> For the bodies of those animals, whose blood is brought into the sanctuary by the high priest for sin, are burned outside the camp. Therefore Jesus also, that He might sanctify the people with His own blood, suffered outside the gate. Therefore let us go forth to Him, outside the camp, bearing His reproach (Hebrews 13:11-13, NKJV).

I have never heard a sermon or a reflection on this passage. The writer here makes a homiletical application of the ritual of the earthly sanctuary. In the book of Leviticus (chapters 4 and 6), we learn that the sin offering was to be handled in one of two ways. Either the blood was to be brought into the Holy Place and sprinkled on the golden altar, or the flesh was to be cooked and a portion eaten by the priest. When the former ritual was followed—the blood carried into the sanctuary—the body of the animal was to be taken outside the camp and burned.

"Outside the camp": the expression occurs several times in Numbers and Deuteronomy. "Outside the camp" was a place of uncleanness, a place to which lepers were banished and where criminals roamed.

Then the author of Hebrews drives home the point: Jesus died "outside the gate." He did not die on the Temple Mount, in the place consecrated for the sanctuary ritual. No! Jesus died in an unholy place, in an unclean place where criminals were executed.

Now, says the Scripture, let us go to Him outside the camp! That is where He is, not in the Holy City, not on the Temple Mount. By planting His Cross outside the gate—outside the camp—our Lord has abolished the old distinctions of clean and unclean, of sacred and profane. No place is off-limits to Him. He is Lord of all. Including the public square.

The Word of the Lord calls us to leave our comfort zones and go where Jesus has gone before: outside the camp, into the public square.

And as we do so, let us be ready to leave the comfort zone of our minds and be open to the new, the big, and the bold. I believe the Lord has given to this church ideas and values that are right for the times. Will we follow Jesus outside the camp?

CHAPTER THREE

Waiting for Jesus:
The *When* or the *Who*?

You will not be able to say that He will come in one, two, or five years, neither are you to put off His coming by stating that it will not be for ten or twenty years. —Ellen White, 1891

A T THE RECENT GENERAL CONFERENCE Session, a refrain heard frequently from the podium was "Jesus may come back before the next Session," or "This is the last General Conference Session that will ever be held."

Nothing new here—I heard the same words at every one of the seven Sessions I attended. Perhaps all that differed was the intensity with which the idea of the imminent return of Jesus was embraced by delegates and visitors. It became a mantra.

Anything wrong in this? Didn't it get people's attention? Doesn't emphasis on Jesus' soon appearing bring excitement?

Yes, but not for a lot of Adventists. When they hear someone say that our Lord will come back before the next General Conference Session—within the next five years—they say to themselves, "I've heard that song before. In fact, I've been hearing it for the past 10 (or 20 or 30 or 40 or 50) years. It's an old familiar score. But we're still here."

Playing the imminence game can be exciting—for a while. But it can also lead to burn-out—eschatological burn-out. There are thousands—only the Lord knows how many—of former Adventists or listless current members, inert to the blessed hope, who have simply given up on the Second Coming.

There is a better way than beating the drum of time. Fasten your seatbelt: our obsession with time, in our past and still today, isn't what our Lord wants.

It's not Jesus' eschatology.

It's not New Testament eschatology.

It's not Ellen White's eschatology.

This may shock you. Consider carefully what I write; I invite you to prove me wrong. But first let's go back to our beginning and in broad strokes trace our history as an apocalyptic movement.

Tracing Our Apocalyptic History

Some 170 years ago a group of men and women in America banded together in quest of a dream. They believed that they would see Jesus Christ coming in the clouds. They were absolutely sure that they were correct. Some abandoned all plans for the future; some left their crops to rot in the ground; all were convinced that the world was about to end.

They were wrong.

Out of that band of broken men and women arose the Seventh-day Adventist Church. The Seventh-day Adventist Church—no longer setting a date for Jesus to appear, but convinced that the big event would take place soon, during their lifetime.

It did not.

Not in their lifetime.

Not in their children's lifetime.

Not in their grandchildren's lifetime.

Not in their great-grandchildren's lifetime.

Can we still dream the dream of Jesus' soon return? Or has the cognitive dissonance reached a degree where we must, in all honesty, step back and re-evaluate?

This church, springing from a dream, has grown and flourished on dreams. In this respect it is by no means unique: behind every enterprise that has left its mark on the world—be it a business, university, hospital, or church—search and you will find that someone or some group had a dream.

So Adventists, dreaming the impossible dream of the imminent *parousia*, also dreamed other dreams, related dreams

—of the gospel going to all the world;

—of clinics and hospitals and medical and dental schools;

—of elementary schools, academies, colleges, and universities.

We were, we are, the doers. We are, as H. Richard Monroe, former chair of Time Inc., described us, the over-achievers. We have never had enough money to start up, never enough to keep going, but we do anyway. We have brought into being a global network of educational and health-care institutions.

What dreamers we have been!

—John Harvey Kellogg, eccentric genius;

—Fernando and Ana Stahl, changing the society of the Altiplano peoples of Peru;

—Ellen White, recognized by *Smithsonian* magazine as one of the 100 most significant Americans of all time;

—W. W. Prescott, educator extraordinary, founding Union College and Walla Walla College (and serving as president of both simultaneously), as well as Battle Creek College;

—Barry Black, rear admiral of the United States Navy, shattering racial stereotypes, chaplain of the US Senate.

And so on and on. Women and men of courage. Of determination. Of vision.

Dreamers all.

Like John Burden and Anna Knight and Leonard Bailey, H. M. S. Richards and Bill Loveless and Roy Branson.

But, can we still dream?

It's a great story, the story of Adventism, the story of our church. But just step back a moment, cast your eye over the picture I just sketched, and consider:

The pioneers of Adventism believed and preached that Jesus was coming soon. But almost from the beginning they began to act in ways that suggested that "soon" wasn't really *so* soon:

—they bought a printing press;

—they established a publishing house;

—they incorporated;

—they organized.

If Jesus is coming within five years, why go to the trouble?

And not only that:

—they married;

—they had children.

If you believe that a time of terrible trouble is about to burst over the world, isn't it irresponsible to produce kids and expose them to it?

And the story goes on:

—they established a school;

—they established a health institute;

—they established a college.

Why, if Jesus is coming within five years, would you do this?

By the turn of the 20th century, we had not one college but a string of them. The publishing work was now housed in a big building in Battle Creek, and it turned out a lot of printing—of all sorts. And we now had built a second publishing house. And now we had a very large health-care institute, famous across America and even abroad, that attracted to its doors the rich and the famous—politicians and presidents, sports stars, the wealthy and the elite of society.

Remember, Ellen White lived through all this dramatic expansion. Ellen White counseled in favor of the expansion.

And Ellen and James had four children of their own.

These facts make the refrain, "This may be the last General Conference Session on earth," seem incongruous. There is a massive disconnect here, a huge cognitive dissonance.

During Ellen White's long career as a messenger to the Seventh-day Adventist Church, from time to time individuals arose among us who declared that Jesus was about to appear. They produced calculations and private interpretations of prophecy. And every time they appeared Ellen rebuked them strongly, warning Adventists not to go down that excitement road.

No more time message, she counseled: "There will never again be a message for the people of God that will be based on time. We are not to know the definite time either for the outpouring of the Holy

Spirit or for the coming of Christ" (*Selected Messages*, Book 1, p. 188).

Shortly before leaving the United States for Australia, Ellen preached at Lansing, Michigan. For her sermon, delivered September 5, 1891, she chose as a key passage Acts 1:3-7, where the disciples asked the risen Lord if He was about to restore the kingdom to Israel. Jesus did not answer their question; instead He said: "It is not for you to know the times or the seasons, which the Father hath put in his own power" (v. 7). These words of Jesus became the theme of Ellen's sermon that day.

> Instead of living in expectation of some special season of excitement we are wisely to improve present opportunities, doing that which must be done in order that souls may be saved. Instead of exhausting the powers of our mind in speculations in regard to the times and seasons which the Lord has placed in His own power, and withheld from men, we are to yield ourselves to the control of the Holy Spirit, to do present duties, to give the bread of life, unadulterated with human opinions, to souls who are perishing for the truth (*Selected Messages*, Book 1, p. 186).

Later in the sermon, she became specific: "You will not be able to say that He will come in one, two, or five years, neither are you to put off His coming by stating that it may not be for ten or twenty years" (p. 189).

Ellen White's counsel still corrects today's church. If we will heed it, we will cease the cries of "Jesus may come before the next General Conference Session" or any other statement that implies that He is about to appear. Instead of focusing on time, we should focus on

Jesus; instead of on the when, on the Who.

This will be very hard for us to do. The time mantra has become ingrained in Adventist thinking. We should proclaim the return of Jesus—proclaim it vigorously, proclaim it joyfully—but we should desist from emphasizing the time aspect.

An example from ancient times, when I was a student studying for the ministry at Avondale College in Australia: It's 1959, and a visiting preacher is giving the Sabbath sermon. He takes up the story of Noah and how he preached for 120 years before the Flood. "Look," says the preacher, "Noah preached for 120 years and then the Flood came. We Adventists have been preaching since 1844. Add 120 years and you arrive at 1964."

"I'm not setting a date for the end of the world," he said. But he was. His whole sermon was built on time, not on Jesus. Without the time aspect his sermon would have fallen apart.

It's a blatant example, but that sort of preaching and writing often has characterized our eschatology. Time to abandon it; time to highlight the Who instead of the when.

What about the Bible? What instruction does our Lord give us about how we should await His coming? What about the New Testament writers?

Jesus' Counsel About Waiting

The Sermon on the Mount, found in Matthew chapters 5-7, is rightly considered the high point of Jesus' teaching. It has been called the Magna Carta of the kingdom of God; it is always included in anthologies of the world's great religious writings. Mahatma Gandhi liked to quote it in his prayer meetings.

In this classic of the Christian life, how much emphasis does Jesus give to waiting for His return? None. Search through the sermon and you can find only three words that come close: "Thy kingdom come" (Matthew 6:10), a prayer that God will bring His rule to earth, ending the long night of sin and darkness.

But there's the long discourse on the End in Matthew 24 (also Mark 13 and Luke 21). Here the Lord, in responding to the disciples' enquiry about when the destruction of Jerusalem will occur and what will be the sign of His coming, gives a sweeping glimpse into the future, a panorama that encompasses in broad strokes the period between that evening on the Mount of Olives and the Second Coming. There will be earthquakes and famines, He tells them, wars and rumors of war, false prophets and false Christs, terrible persecution along with the gospel of the kingdom spreading to all the world.

He will come back, and that coming will catch many people asleep at the switch, drunk to the signs of the times. So His followers are to keep alert, doing their appointed work faithfully and ready to greet the Master when He appears.

In this major presentation on the End, we do not find any hint of excitement, of a five-year window in which Jesus will return. Rather, the opposite: Jesus tells us that no one, not even the angels, can know just when He will come again.

The Gospel of John, as in so many other areas, has a different take on the Second Coming from what we find in Mathew, Mark, and Luke. There is no apocalyptic discourse, but we do find the words so precious to Adventists: "I will come again, and receive you unto myself" (John 14:3). The emphasis, however, falls not on signs of the End as in Matthew 24 and parallels, but on the Holy Spirit. Jesus is about to leave His disciples and return to the Father, but He promises: "I will not leave you as orphans; I will come to you.... But the Advocate, the Holy Spirit, whom the Father will send in My name, will teach you all things and will remind you of everything I have said to you" (John 14:18, 26, NIV). This theme of the coming of the Holy Spirit dominates John 14-17.

In the final chapter of John's Gospel we read of a fascinating incident among the followers of Jesus. The risen Lord and His followers are by the Sea of Galilee. Peter asks Jesus what is to happen to the Beloved Disciple and Jesus replies, "If I want him to remain alive until I return, what is that to you? You must follow me" (John 21:22, NIV). Then John, writing as an old man with the rest of the Twelve all gone, comments: "Because of this, the rumor spread among the believers that this disciple would not die. But Jesus did not say that he would not die; he only said, 'If I want him to remain alive until I return, what is that to you?'" (v. 23).

We can imagine the scenario: The apostles become fewer and fewer, as one by one they meet a martyr's death. Now only John remains of the Twelve, and he is an old man. How much longer can he go on? Surely Jesus is coming very soon!

A message based on time.

They are wrong. John died. And Jesus didn't return.

The entire New Testament, every book, throbs with the glad certainty of the Second Coming. It is the "blessed hope" of all who love the Lord. But that hope means a patient waiting, a waiting in hope, a waiting in trust. A waiting that obeys Jesus' words: "You must follow me," rather than one that drums up excitement because it has convinced itself that the time is very short.

The Delay

Reinforcing unhealthy excitement over an imminent Second

Coming is the idea that Jesus could have come and should have come ere this. Books, articles, and sermons have assumed that the Lord's return has been delayed and have attempted to explain why.

Here theologians as diverse in their thinking as Herbert Douglass and Desmond Ford find common ground. For Douglass, the "harvest principle" was key: Jesus waits until the harvest is ripe, meaning until God's people have attained the character He requires. For Ford, the reason for the delay is found in the gospel—the true gospel of righteousness by faith proclaimed in power will sweep the world and Jesus will come. That could have happened in the first century AD; it could still happen.

So ingrained has the "delay" idea become in the thinking of many Adventists that it is shocking to discover that it cannot be supported by the New Testament data. The tenor of biblical thought runs directly counter to it.

Search the pages of the New Testament; you won't find this theology at all. Only in one place do you hear someone stating, "My master is delaying his coming" (Luke 12:45, NKJV), but that comes from the wicked servant, not one of God's faithful ones! So if we sound the "delay" refrain, we are in undesirable company!

Throughout the Bible, God is set forth as Lord of time and space. One "who's got the whole world in His hands." God gives human beings the freedom to choose, but not to frustrate His will. To suggest that Jesus could have returned nearly 2,000 years ago if His followers had done their job flies in the face of Scripture—it is incongruent with the biblical picture of God.

We have fallen into an eschatology by works: we would make the Lord dependent on us. We do not, cannot, bring on the Second Coming. "God will bring [it] about in his own time—God, the blessed and only Ruler, the King of kings and Lord of lords" (1 Timothy 6:15, NIV).

Another common Adventist expression is "finishing the work," meaning that we finish the Gospel work so the Lord can return. But what does Scripture tell us? "He [God] will finish the work, and cut it short in righteousness" (Romans 9:28). He, not us. We have a part to play, but God is Lord of the mission.

Out of the thousands of verses in the Bible, one—just one—suggests that we can affect the time of Jesus' return: "Since everything will be destroyed in this way, what kind of people ought you to be? You ought to live holy and godly lives as you look forward to the day of God and speed its coming." (2 Peter 3:11-12, NIV). That passage, however, speaks not of our delaying the Second Coming but rather of hastening it!

How Then Shall We Live?

In joyful, confident expectation of Jesus' return.

In living to His glory, perfecting holiness in the fear of God.

In continuing the teaching and healing ministry of Jesus, as by word and by life we spread the good news.

In calm, peaceful waiting every day.

Paul tells us: "But when the set time had fully come, God sent his Son" (Galatians 4:4, NIV). God sent Him once in the fullness of time, and He will send Him again when the time has fully come.

Yes, He will come, as He promised. The Cross guarantees the cloud. "Like the stars in the vast circuit of their appointed path, God's purposes know no haste and no delay" (*The Desire of Ages*, p. 32).

CHAPTER FOUR

The Message:
Will We Keep the Main Thing
the Main Thing?

The main thing is to keep the main thing the main thing.
—Steven Covey

WHAT IS OUR MESSAGE TO GIVE to the world? Is it something altogether new in Christian history?

Back in the days when I taught at Spicer Memorial College in India (now Spicer Adventist University), a missionary arrived to present the annual Week of Prayer. He built his sermons around the theme of Righteousness by Faith, leading us day by day through the biblical stories of Abraham, David, and so on. It was, overall, a good week, helpful and encouraging—until his final message on Sabbath morning. For some reason he used the occasion to attack the wearing of wedding bands.

In India married women indicate their status by one or more wedding signs. Some wear a ring, but in other parts of the country a gold chain—called a thali—is worn around the neck. For still others, a bangle or bangles worn on the wrist announces that a woman is married. Some women wear more than one wedding sign.

Long before Noelene and I arrived in India as young missionaries, leaders of the Adventist church discussed the prevailing customs and arrived at a standard for church members: any one of the wedding signs—ring, thali, or bangle—but not more than one.

The presenter, having spent many years in India, surely knew the policy of the Adventist church. But he had a "burden" about the matter: any and all wedding bands were wrong! And so—can you believe it?—he brought the series on righteousness by faith to a climax by making an altar call for the people to come forward renouncing the wedding sign!

Unbelievable! What a travesty of the gospel.

As I recall, the response from the audience was tepid: a handful of compliant students and staff shuffled to the front. The president of the college was furious, as was his spouse, who wore a thali. I went home shaking my head.

The good brother, an earnest and devout servant of the Lord, drew his convictions from a few brief comments in the writings of Ellen White. Those comments were directed to Adventists in North America and were written in the context of avoiding wasteful spending. She made it clear that she had no wish to impose the counsel on the church in other lands.

An extreme example perhaps, but not uncommon. Long-time Adventists reading this book will recall other instances of a similar vein.

So just what is our message to the world? More than wedding bands and bangles, I hope.

And is our message *sui generis*, the only one of its kind, something unique to us, something that Luther, Calvin, Wesley, and the other Reformers did not and could not know?

Let's take a quick look at the Adventist message over the course of our history. Then we'll go back to where we must—to the Bible—to find what our message ought to be.

The Message Over the Years

Early Adventist preachers, feeling called to declare the importance of the Sabbath, tended to focus on the law rather than the gospel. They preached the law to such an extent that Ellen White stated that their sermons "were as dry as the hills of Gilboa" (*Review and Herald*, March 11, 1890). Matters came to a head at the General Conference Session of 1888, held in Minneapolis, Minnesota. Two young ministers, Ellet J. Waggoner and Alonzo T. Jones, sounded the theme of righteousness by faith alone. Leaders of the church, thinking that this emphasis weakened the arguments for the law and Sabbath, opposed them strongly. So Waggoner and Jones stood alone against George I. Butler, the president of the General Conference, Uriah Smith, editor of the *Review and Herald*, as well as other stalwarts.

Not quite alone! One leader publicly espoused the cause. Ellen G. White, in a sad turn of events, found her counsel rejected.

But the gospel was unstoppable, just as it has been in every age. Following the 1888 Session, especially under Ellen White's leadership by pen and voice, the message of righteousness by faith slowly advanced, wider and wider, further and further until it became an established teaching of the Seventh-day Adventist Church.

Ellen White penned some of the loveliest expressions of the gospel that can be found anywhere. Echoing Isaiah's prophecy of the Suffering Servant, she wrote:

> Christ was treated as we deserve, that we might be treated as He deserves. He was condemned for our sins, in which He had no share, that we might be justified by His righteousness, in which we had no share. He suffered the death which was ours, that we might receive the life which was His. "With His stripes we are healed" (*The Desire of Ages*, p. 25).

Commenting on Jesus' parable of the man without a wedding garment, she noted:

> Only the covering which Christ Himself has provided can make us meet to appear in God's presence. This covering, the robe of His own righteousness, Christ will put upon every repenting, believing soul. "I counsel thee," He says, "to buy of Me . . . white raiment, that thou mayest be clothed, and that the shame of thy nakedness do not appear." Revelation 3:18.
>
> This robe, woven in the loom of heaven, has in it not one thread of human devising (*Christ's Object Lessons*, p. 311).

During Adventism's struggle over the gospel, editor Uriah Smith wrote a series of editorials in the *Review* in which he argued that we need Christ's righteousness to be justified, but after we accept Christ we must develop a righteousness of our own by keeping the law. Ellen White rebuked him sharply in a letter. She stated that she had read Smith's editorial and that a "noble personage" had stood beside her and told her that Uriah Smith "is walking like a blind man into the prepared net of the enemy, but he feels no danger because light is becoming darkness to him and darkness light" (Letter 55, 1889).

Of all Ellen White's numerous gems on righteousness by faith, here is my favorite: "To him who is content to receive without deserving, who feels that he can never recompense such love, who lays all doubt and unbelief aside, and comes as a little child to the feet of Jesus, all the treasures of eternal love are a free, everlasting gift" (Letter 19e-1892, Oct. 26, 1892).

In every age the gospel has seemed too good to be true. Whenever it is proclaimed it arouses opposition, just as it did when Paul brought it to the Galatians. Not surprisingly, therefore, Adventist history presents a mixed picture with regard to righteousness by faith.

Thus, even after 1888 and Ellen White's strong counsel regarding the once-for-all, all-sufficiency of Christ's death for our sins, one finds from time to time attempts to add to the simple gospel. These efforts sometimes run along the lines of Uriah Smith's argument quoted above—that Christ's death justified us, but after that our works are necessary to live the sanctified life.

Another position, one that goes back as far as the late M. L. Andreassen, emphasizes the righteousness that must be had by those redeemed from the earth when Jesus returns. This "last generation" theology focuses on perfection of character rather than righteousness by faith. In doing so it falls into the error that Paul addressed in his letter to the Galatians, namely, adding something to the gospel, which declares that Christ has done it all for us.

In view of our checkered history, what should be our message for the world today?

The Main Thing

"The main thing is to keep the main thing the main thing," wrote Steven Covey, author of *The Seven Habits of Highly Effective People*, which sold more than 25 million copies.

Not one thing among others, not second most important, but the main thing.

The apostle Paul tells us what the main thing is. Writing to the believers in Corinth about 25 years after Jesus died, he says:

Look at the Revised version

> Now, brothers and sisters, I want to remind you of the gospel I preached to you, which you received and on which you have taken your stand. By this gospel you are saved, if you hold firmly to the word I preached to you. Otherwise, you have believed in vain. For what I received I passed on to you as of first importance: that Christ died for our sins according to the Scriptures (1 Corinthians 15:1-3, NIV).

Paul here is nearing the conclusion of a long letter. He has dealt with many topics—with divisions and factions in the congregation, with a blatant case of immorality (a man had taken his father's wife as his sexual partner), with meat that had been offered to idols before being sold in the market, with questions of marital relations, with disorderly conduct at the Lord's Supper, with misuse of spiritual gifts, and so on.

Now as he completes the letter, Paul doesn't mention any of these topics. Instead he reminds them of the main thing—the gospel.

"By this gospel," he says, "you are saved." And by this gospel we are saved. It is the main thing. It is of first importance.

The Corinthians needed reminding. We also need reminding.

We Seventh-day Adventists are great at dreaming up new plans and programs. Too often we're driven by finding a plan that will, as we like to say, "finish the work." Jesus hasn't come back as we think He should have. In one way or another we're to blame, so we need to hit on the answer—we need one more program, the one program that will wrap it up, and then we'll see Jesus coming in the clouds.

Believe me, I'm not exaggerating. I spent 25 years at the GC and the leaders there—for the most part dedicated, earnest men and women—spend much of that time creating new programs.

But we're still here. After thousands of plans and programs, after a ton of money spent trying to make them work, we're still here!

What went wrong?

What is still wrong?

Looking back on those years, I have to ask: was our failure in not keeping the main thing the main thing? *To me, this question just encourages the idea that we spend God's coming*

Paul was sure about the main thing; he wasn't confused. But what about us? *Are we confused?*

What do Adventists think is the main thing?

The Sabbath, because it sets us apart? Our pioneers hammered the Sabbath; they beat up on Sunday-keeping clergy in debates. And the Sabbath is important: it's God's gift to humanity, needed today more than ever. But the Sabbath, important as it is, isn't the main thing. Not according to Paul: it's not there in his list of "first importance."

The Second Coming? Another teaching of great importance, the "blessed hope" assures us that this messed-up world isn't the last word, that God hasn't abandoned us and left us to wander on, groping in darkness and fear. Jesus is coming again!

But the Second Coming, so dear to us, isn't the main thing, although for a lot of Adventists it is. They spend hours and hours trying to figure out just when Jesus will return, although He told us that no one, not even the angels, knows the time. Some of us focus on the events of the last days, the calamities, the persecution, the "time of trouble."

And thereby they miss the main thing.

Well, the three angels' messages? That's our commission, our marching orders. Doesn't the Lord want us to go beyond Martin Luther and the Reformers to give the final message to a dying world?

Not so fast. Look at Revelation 14 again and there, right at the beginning of the three angels' messages, you find that it's the "eternal gospel" that is to go to every nation, tribe, language and people" (v. 6).

That means the main thing for us is the same as it was for the believers in Corinth 2,000 years ago.

I had a good, long inning as editor of the *Adventist Review*. I used to get a lot of letters, most of them affirming, some a bit nasty, and some so hot that you needed asbestos gloves to handle them! And every now and then there'd be a letter in which the writer said that God had given them a message for the church and that it was to be printed in the *Review* at once! And warning me that if I didn't publish it, God would let me have it!

So much misguided effort: calculations and charts, compilations from Ellen White, stuff, stuff, stuff.

And all missing the first importance. All that without realizing that the main thing is to keep the main thing the main thing.

What is the Main Thing?

Paul tells us, and it's simple. You don't need a doctoral degree to get it. You don't need to go to the Seminary to find it.

The main thing, the matter of first importance, comes to just five little words: "Christ died for our sins." Five little words, but loaded with meaning. Five little words, but they are the gospel. Five little words, but they tell us the meaning of the death of Jesus of Nazareth.

CHRIST: To the Roman soldiers, Jesus' death was just one more execution of a troublemaker. Another day, another loser.

Crucifixion was Rome's brutal method of handling dissenters. They stretched them out on two wooden beams and nailed or tied their wrists and ankles. Then they lifted the cross with the body hanging from it and dropped it into a hole. The victim hung there, helpless, unable to move or to brush off flies or ants that gathered around the blood. It was a slow, agonizing way to die; it sometimes took days.

And always it was public. Rome wanted to send a message, loud and clear, to anyone who entertained ideas of revolt: This is what you can expect. So, on Jesus' cross, over His head, they wrote: "Jesus of Nazareth the King of the Jews" (John 19:19). In the accounts of the crucifixion in the four Gospels, the wording varies slightly, but all include "the King of the Jews."

King of the Jews—mocking, taunting.

King of the Jews—warning, watch out.

Pilate wrote "Jesus," but Paul says, "Christ." To the Romans, the man on the middle cross was only that, a man, a human being. But to Paul and to us He is more. He is the Christ, the Anointed One, the Messiah.

When at Caesarea Philippi, Jesus asked His disciples, "Who do you say I am?" Peter in a flash of inspiration replied, "You are the Messiah, the Son of the living God" (Matthew 16:16, NIV). He was. He is.

That's where the gospel begins. That's how the main thing starts: "Christ." Not just a man, although He was truly human. Not just a good man. Not just the best man who ever lived—the purest, the kindest, the noblest. He was all this, but He was more.

Sometimes this life of ours, beautiful as it is, seems almost too much to bear. We get cancer, or we see a loved one get cancer and we suffer with them. We lose our job. Our marriage that started so wonderfully goes sour. We find ourselves treated unfairly, unjustly. People at church are mean to us. We wonder: How can I cope? How can I go on living?

We want to cry out, "Why, God? I didn't ask to be born. Why are you doing this to me? God, if you are God, you owe me an apology."

But then we come to Calvary. We see a Man hanging on the cross in the center. We hear Him cry out, "Why?" And that one "Why" answers all our "whys." The inscription on His cross reads "Jesus," but He isn't just Jesus, the child of Mary. He is the Christ, the Messiah, the Son of the living God.

Then it hits us: God doesn't owe us an apology. We owe God an apology! I don't get this

DIED: The main thing, the first importance, says Paul, the gospel, is: Christ died for our sins.

Not: Christ lived a perfect life. But: Christ died for our sins.

Never did another person live such a life. He is our Example. But the gospel tells us that before we talk about Christ as our Example, before anything else we say about Him, He died. *Suggest the Life? the writ doesn't matter*

Look at the four stories about Jesus of Nazareth, the Gospels: Matthew, Mark, Luke, and John. Sometimes they're called "Lives" of Jesus, but they aren't. They are all really "Deaths" of Jesus, with extended introductions.

Matthew has 28 chapters, but the last eight of them—about 30 percent—focus on the final week of Jesus' of Nazareth.

Is the reason there is more about the death of christ then the life really because that is more important or because it would be impossible to record it.?

[handwritten: Could part of this be because they were not with him during the earlier parts of his life.]

Mark has only 16 chapters in all, and the final six chapters, three-eighths of the book, deal with the Passion.

In Luke the numbers are 24 and six—one quarter of this Gospel focuses on the last events of Jesus' earthly existence.

In the Gospel of John the emphasis on Jesus' death is even greater: no fewer than 10 chapters out of the 21 take up the Passion. That's almost one-half of the entire book! [handwritten: Juvenile argument]

If you set out to write a biography of Abraham Lincoln and you ended up giving about 50 percent of the book to the events surrounding Lincoln's assassination by John Wilkes Booth in Ford's Theater, what would the reviewers say? "You didn't write a biography of Lincoln—you wrote about the death of Lincoln."

Matthew, Mark, Luke, and John got it. They got the gospel. The main thing, the first importance, is Christ's death. [handwritten: Really?]

All the writers of the New Testament follow the same pattern. Search through it and, apart from the four Gospels, you find hardly any references to the life of Jesus of Nazareth. Given the attention we tend to give to that marvelous life, the silence seems extraordinary. But what you do find, in every book from Acts to Revelation, is a constant refrain on the death of Christ. They all, along with Matthew, Mark, Luke, and John, play the same tune. Their violin has only one string. [handwritten: Maybe because they are going off of what they have.]

What is going on? They're keeping the main thing the main thing.

But why this focus on death? Why did Jesus keep coming back to it as He and the disciples made their final journey from Galilee to Jerusalem? "We are going up to Jerusalem,' he said, 'and the Son of Man will be delivered over to the chief priests and the teachers of the law. They will condemn him to death and will hand him over to the Gentiles, who will mock him and spit on him, flog him and kill him.

Three days later he will rise'" (Mark 10:33-34, NIV).

His words carry a note of inevitability: His destiny is to die. He will die in Jerusalem, not just because He posed a threat to both the Romans and the Jewish Establishment, but because it is His destiny, His role in a divine plan. So on the road to Emmaus the Sunday morning of the Resurrection, He rebuked Cleopas and his companion for their failure to understand the Scriptures, and asked rhetorically, "Did not the Messiah have to suffer these things and then enter his glory?" (Luke 24:26, NIV).

"It's already there—in the Scriptures," He was saying. Already the Old Testament focuses on the death of Messiah.

Where? In the rituals around which the spiritual life of Israel was centered—the death of animals. The Old Testament is awash with blood. Read through the book of Leviticus and what do you find? Ritual after ritual, slaughter after slaughter. The priests who ministered at the sanctuary were like holy butchers.

Of course all this slaughter, all this blood, in itself couldn't make people better. Sin is a moral problem—it can't be made right by killing an animal. Suppose I get angry and hit someone so that he dies. How can I fix the problem? Slaughter a sheep or a goat? Now we have a dead man as well as a dead sheep or goat!

This is why the book of Hebrews, which deals in detail with the Old Testament sanctuary, tells us unequivocally: "It is impossible for the blood of bulls and goats to take away sins" (Hebrews 10:4, NIV). But it goes on to argue that there is a sacrifice that takes away sins, even the sacrifice of Jesus. Just one sacrifice. One, for all people, for all time: "So Christ was sacrificed once to take away the sins of many; and he will appear a second time, not to bear sin, but to bring salvation to those who are waiting for him" (Hebrews 9:28, NIV).

Here, in Hebrews, we look deeply into the mystery of the Man on the cross. Why did He die? Why did He have to die? What was all this slaughter of animals under the old sanctuary all about? The author of Hebrews tells us. "Without the shedding of blood there is no forgiveness" (Hebrews 9:22, NIV).

Now we begin to grasp it: God's way of making matters right leads through death. Without shedding of blood, no forgiveness. Without the death of Christ, no gospel.

Let's be clear on one thing. God isn't a vengeful deity that demands blood. No! Just the opposite! God takes upon Himself our death: He dies on a cross.

FOR OUR SINS: In the 53rd chapter of Isaiah we find a profound scene. We see the mysterious figure of the Suffering Servant who will be the divine Agent of redemption:

But he was pierced for our transgressions,
  he was crushed for our iniquities;
the punishment that brought us peace was on him,
  and by his wounds we are healed.
We all, like sheep, have gone astray,
  each of us has turned to our own way;
and the Lord has laid on him
  the iniquity of us all (Isaiah 53:5-6, NIV).

Then, the final verses of Isaiah 53:

He poured out his life unto death,
  and was numbered with the transgressors.
For he bore the sin of many

and made intercession for the transgressors (v. 12).

Going back to Paul: "Christ died for our sins." And then, writing to the Corinthians:

God made him who had no sin to be sin [or a sin offering] for us, so that in him we might become the righteousness of God (2 Corinthians 5:21).

This is the main thing. Always has been. Always will be. Don't try to add anything to it, because then it won't be the main thing.

Change one of these five little words. Instead of "our" read "my": Christ died for my sins.

All my failures. All the times I've messed up. All my broken promises. All my pride. All my envy. All my selfishness. All my thoughtlessness. All my meanness. All my neglect. All my missed opportunities to do good, to help others.

Christ died for my sins.

He did. It's real. It's true.

It's liberating. It's the door to new life, to laughter, to singing, to creativity, to freedom.

The Gospel of John

Now there remains just one aspect of Jesus' death for us to consider. Paul tells us that the main thing, the first importance, "that Christ died for our sins" was according to the Scriptures.

The death of Jesus was a bloody, agonizing crucifixion. It was, but it was more. It was "according to the Scriptures."

This was no chance death, no accident of history. Jesus of Nazareth didn't happen to be in the wrong place at the wrong time. No, everything that happened to Him was "according to the Scriptures." Back of Pilate and Caiaphas, back of all the intrigue and treachery, was God. God working through it all, working out a plan to save the world.

The Gospel of John gives us insight into what was happening behind the scenes. This Gospel, written last of the four, probably 30 or so years after the others, shows deep reflection on the meaning of Jesus' death. What emerges is not a picture that contradicts what we find in Matthew, Mark, and Luke, but rather one that enormously enriches the perspective that we find in their accounts.

John's Gospel, as we noted already, is dominated by our Lord's Passion, and in a startling new way. Instead of dwelling on the tragedy and suffering of the Cross, John sees it now in glowing terms, positive terms. For Him, the death of Christ for our sins is covered in glory. *What does Glory mean?*

That word, glory, is key to understanding the Gospel of John. We find it early in the prologue: "The Word became flesh and made his dwelling among us. We have seen his glory, the glory of the one and only Son, who came from the Father full of grace and truth" (John 1:14, NIV). We find it again in the second chapter, when John recounts the story of the wedding feast in Cana and notes: "What Jesus did here in Cana of Galilee was the first of the signs through which he revealed his glory; and his disciples believed in him" (John 2:11, NIV).

Altogether we find in John "glory" or "glorify," mentioned some 40 times. Most occurrences come during the Passion week. Throughout His ministry Jesus looks ahead to what He calls "my hour," telling His disciples that His hour has not yet arrived. Then at last in Jerusalem He says: "The hour has come for the Son of Man to be glorified" (John 12:23, NIV). He prays to God: "Father, glorify your name!" and a voice comes from heaven, "I have glorified it, and will glorify it again" (John 12:28, NIV).

At the Cross much more is happening than meets the eye of the passersby who out of morbid curiosity have come out to see three men die. More than they see; more than the soldiers see as they sit playing dice. At the Cross a fierce, unseen battle is being waged. The forces of evil are making their final assault on God and His government. The assault comes with all the weapons of the Prince of Darkness—the lie, the torture, the agony. And the forces of good take it on the chin. They don't reply in kind: instead of the lie, truth; instead of force, suffering; instead of hate, love.

Jesus of Nazareth died on a Roman cross.

Christ died for our sins according to the Scriptures.

And it is glorious. Glorious with the glory that shines from the face of God.

My friends, this is God's testimony about Jesus. It is my testimony, but don't accept it just because of me. Believe it, accept it because it is God's testimony about His Son.

"Christ died for our sins according to the Scriptures."

This is the main thing. This is our message for the world, to be preached in this End time.

"The last rays of merciful light, the last message of mercy to be given to the world, is a revelation of His character of love" (*Christ's Object Lessons*, p. 415).

[handwritten margin notes: "Isn't it Christ's testimony about God?"; "How do we understand this?"; "God's or Christ's?"; "Who's character of love is White referring to here? Christ's or God's or are they the same?"]

CHAPTER FIVE

Organization:
Thinking the Unthinkable

We must dare to think "unthinkable" thoughts.
We must learn to explore all the options and possibilities
that confront us in a complex and rapidly changing world.
—J. William Fulbright

CHANGES ARE COMING IN ADVENTIST church structure—big changes. The changes are inevitable, but the question is: Will we see what lies ahead and be bold enough to make adjustments, or will we be overtaken—not to say overwhelmed—by the tsunami of change?

I am not the first person to address this topic. For more than 30 years historian George Knight, in articles, books, and public addresses, has sounded a prophetic call for change. Relentlessly he has pointed out that the church has become too ponderous to fulfill its mission. His "The Fat Lady and the Kingdom," originally published in the *Adventist Review* in 1991, was later reprinted in a book with the same title (1995). In another provocatively titled work, *If I Were the Devil* (2007), Knight expanded on the same theme.

Other voices, particularly in North America, have drawn attention in recent years to trends that will have a major impact on our church.

Very few people, Adventists included, welcome change. Many readers will find this chapter disquieting, even alarming. But I think the writing is on the wall—to use a biblical metaphor. Too many bits of evidence make it abundantly clear that we won't be able to sustain the organization that has served us well for a century. The realities of the world church—numbers, makeup, finances—will force major changes in the way we do church.

We Adventists love a good report. We rejoice with the larger, newer, bigger, first. We rise to sing "Praise God from whom all blessings flow." So we find it hard to deal with realities that changing times bring: when the church is declining rather than growing, when we shutter a church, when an institution goes bankrupt. We haven't yet learned to sing the Lord's song in a strange land, as the people of God long before us were forced to do (see Psalm 137).

The Review and Herald

I served on the board of the Review and Herald Publishing Association for 25 years. The publishing house, founded by James White in 1852, was our oldest institution. Located originally in Battle Creek, Michigan, it moved to Washington, DC, along with General Conference headquarters, in 1903. It had become a large, prosperous, flourishing business: it employed hundreds of workers and published high-quality books that an army of colporteurs sold by the thousands, going from door to door, as well as a raft of periodicals that nurtured Adventist life from the cradle to the grave.

By 1980 the plant in Washington, DC, had become obsolete and altogether inadequate for the booming enterprise. "The House" moved out of the city to a rural location some 70 miles away in Hagerstown, Maryland. There, on a spacious green campus, a large state-of-the-art publishing facility rose from the farmland. It was built big enough to supply the publishing needs of the entire world Adventist church.

I joined the board just after the move to Hagerstown. The House printed the *Adventist Review*; I became closely acquainted with the employees who cared for design and layout, copy-editing, printing, and marketing of the many products produced on site. They were a fine team of men and women who gave their best to the work. They believed in the Review and Herald, believed that it was God's publishing house. It was.

To suggest in those days that the publishing house might someday fold was unthinkable. Whatever dire circumstances might arise, the House would survive, because it was the Lord's institution. To the very end, many continued to believe that a way out would emerge and the House would survive.

My experience as a member of the board of the Review and Herald took me through a wide range of emotions. For several years board meetings were largely times of fellowship with members who flew and drove in from around the United Sates. We listened to reports of progress and took home gift copies of new releases, but we conducted little analysis—let alone critical analysis—of the business.

We seemed blissfully unaware of the vast changes in printing and publishing that the digital age was bringing all around us. I recall only one voice that was raised urging the House to diversify, to not rely totally on printing. It came from a well-informed layperson, but he did not get a hearing and was soon dropped from the board. As the years went on, I became more and more uncomfortable with board meetings. The annual reports from the auditors showed a steadily declining bottom line—year after year of red ink. It seemed clear to me that the House was on a course that led to ruin. The board, however, at no time was given opportunity to confront the situation—all discussion of finances was restricted to the Finance Committee of the board.

The Review and Herald was in big trouble. The world had changed: magazines were struggling, going under; on-line was replacing print; city dwellers didn't open their homes to door-to-door salespeople. The finances of the House plummeted. Finally, the sad day came, the unthinkable day in 2014, when the Review and Herald, bankrupt, went out of business and the property was put up for sale.

From this experience I learned this: Take nothing for granted. The future is not assured—not for an Adventist university, college, or academy; not for a hospital or publishing house; not for the General Conference; not for the General Conference Session. I also learned the fallacy of the reasoning that "the Lord won't let it fail." It's dangerous to predict what God will do, to go beyond what He has revealed of His will in Scripture.

A third thing I learned was to beware of the misuse of Ellen White's writings. Her counsels, which I believe were God-inspired, were addressed to specific situations in the life of the Church and so, as she herself directed us, time and place should always be taken into account in seeking to apply them in different situations. For too many Adventists, then and now, however, the Ellen White writings function like a compendium of statements that can be pulled up online, wrenched out of context, and applied in ways she never intended. Thus, among the factors leading to a misguided confidence in the permanence of the Review and Herald was an appeal to isolated statements that appeared to support that conviction.

Three General Conference Presidents—Folkenberg, Paulsen, and Ted Wilson—made attempts to address the growing publishing crisis in North America. The Review and Herald, like Pacific Press, its counterpart in Nampa, Idaho, was a General Conference institution with a General Conference vice president chairing its board. (Pacific Press is now a North American Division institution.) The publishing house on the East coast, larger and overbuilt, was increasingly unprofitable; the other, Pacific Press, smaller and compact, was on a sound business footing. It made sense to merge the two publishing houses, and each of the three Presidents set up a commission to bring this about. All three Presidents failed: vested interests, along with Ellen White quotations, doomed the efforts.

The Review and Herald went under. The church press gave little notice to its demise. The Church at its highest levels would have benefited from a hard-hitting, candid committee of inquiry to analyze what went wrong and what we might learn from the loss of this premier institution. We Adventists find it hard to deal with negative developments.

I felt keenly for the Review and Herald workers. For many of them, the House was their life. They connected with it early, gave their best years to it, established their homes near it, believed in it, and toiled to make it successful. And then the unthinkable happened. Could it all have been handled better—handled in a manner more befitting a Christian institution? I have to think that the answer is Yes, and that is why I am troubled that we may not have learned lessons that the Lord has for us from the loss of the Review and Herald. (I should mention that the Church dealt compassionately with the House employees who were thrust out of work.)

I am "bullish" on the Seventh-day Adventist Church. I rejoice in its remarkable growth, its vigorous mission endeavors, its new hospitals and universities. But I am also realistic. Along with rejoicing comes the sobering, counterweight evidence:

—While the church is surging ahead in some areas, in others it is dying. For Adventists in Western Europe the struggle is one of survival.

—The loss of the Review and Herald is by no means a unique event. For European Adventists, the sale of our premier medical institution, Skodsberg Sanitarium in Denmark, left a bitter taste. In North America, Atlantic Union College fell into financial straits, lost its accreditation, and is struggling to make a comeback. Many church members are alumni of academies that no longer exist.

Times are changing, and the church has to change before change is forced upon us. Can we see what is coming and plan for change? Or will we cling to false dreams and false reasoning until the roof caves in on us?

Facing Reality

The official church press has done little to acquaint Adventists with the realities facing the Church and to help them to cope with the changes that I think are inevitable. A notable exception is an editorial in the South Pacific Division's *Adventist Record* by editor James

Standish immediately following the San Antonio General Conference Session. Simply titled "Thoughts," the editorial candidly addressed several issues concerning how we do church. I reproduce it in full:

"Walking through San Antonio the day after the General Conference Session feels eerily like the day after the apocalypse. The life that appeared so real has vanished. The streets are empty. The booths are dismantled. Silence has descended on the Alamodome. But not for long. Ironically, Mötley Crüe, the heavy metal band from LA, will soon replace the Adventists on the big stage.

"Soon, it will be like we never were here. A blip in time. A bump on the road. An ethereal mist that dissipated.

"There are men and women who left elated. Their views confirmed. Their anointing recognized. Their faith rejuvenated. And I am very, very glad for them. I wish I was one. I'm not.

"I hope you don't mind this level of candor. I also hope you don't mind me sharing my concerns as just one of possibly 18.5 million Adventists.

"I say possibly, as the reports from the GC secretary's team made clear, our membership numbers are so deeply unreliable that all we know for certain is that we have no idea how many members we really have. We have an inbuilt incentive to exaggerate. A disincentive to clean up numbers. And no global independent audit. This produces predictably distorted results.

"One of the incentives to inflate numbers is that the number of delegates does, in part, turn on membership count. But that isn't the only problem in the way delegates are selected. Globally, we desperately need a far more transparent, democratic process for selecting delegates. We also need fewer ex officio delegates. A large number of ex officio delegates are ordained pastors and therefore male. There is something troubling about a room of almost 2600 delegates debating the role of women in the Church, where only 17 per cent of the delegates are women. And the result of the vote, by its nature, ensures that is the way it will likely continue as so many of the ex officio positions are reserved exclusively for the ordained. This produces a self-confirming circularity that is both unwise and unfair.

"Obviously the most divisive issue discussed was the ordination of women. The distinction between the ordination of deacons and elders, and the ordination of pastors, is not biblical; it is administrative. At what point, when we deal with a question that is not a fundamental belief, is not an issue of salvation, where the distinction is administrative and where dedicated, Bible believing, faithful Adventists see things differently, do we agree to respect the conscience of others?

"Which goes to my greater concern—our drift from our radical Reformation roots. We believe God speaks to all. But we voted to shut down the conscience of others. We have no creed but the Bible. But we spent an inordinate amount of time debating jots and tittles in Fundamental Beliefs. As a movement, we are drifting very dangerously into the hierarchicalism, formalism and dogmatism that our pioneers explicitly rejected. As a friend quipped, 'We criticize the Catholics for their traditions and dogmas built up over the 1700 years since Constantine co-opted Christianity, but look how many we've built up just in the last century!'

"Finally, after doing a little number crunching, I came to a rough estimate that it costs in the range of $A30 million for the organized Church and at least another $15 million from associated ministries to stage the GC Session. So that is in the range of $45 million funded by Adventist giving. If we break it down to a per member, per year, over five years basis, that isn't very much. But every GC Session leaves me wondering if this is the best possible way to spend our time, money and energy.

"Imagine if we had a far simpler Session, and every five years we spent $45 million on coordinated evangelism in one of the largest cities in the world. Imagine us competing for souls, rather than positions and donor money. Imagine 60,000 Adventists converging for converting on Paris, Lagos, Shanghai or Melbourne. With a $45 million budget backing us up! Alternatively, imagine us using the $45 million to feed in the range of 25,000 hungry children, every day, for five years. It's our choice. And I have to wonder what Christ would have us do?

"I love our Church. I love it enough to take the career risk to talk openly about my concerns. And enough to do my best to be part of the solution to them."

Time to Rethink: The General Conference Session

So closely has the GC Session become associated with the modern Adventist church that to question it seems almost heresy. But the facts are these: Search the Bible and Ellen White's writings and you cannot find support for the way we conduct General Conference Sessions today. And so changed have the Sessions become that the original purpose is almost lost. It's time to rethink, to consider changing the General Conference Session and the structures of the Church from the top down.

Much can be advanced in support of the current format. If James Standish came away from San Antonio with a bad taste in his mouth, many others who were there had the opposite reaction. They left feeling uplifted—inspired by the feast of musical treats, encouraged by biblical preaching and the hope of the Second Coming that was proclaimed loud and often, glowing with the warmth of Christian fellowship, and proud to be part of something that is BIG, growing, and dynamic.

My first experience with a General Conference Session came during our years as missionaries in India. We were on furlough, studying at the Seminary; it was easy and cost saving for the Southern Asia Division to appoint me as one of the official delegates to the Session, meeting in Cobo Hall in nearby Detroit. After I joined the *Adventist Review* I was appointed as a delegate six Sessions in a row, spanning 30 years. For those Sessions the grind of publishing daily bulletins occupied my time day and night. Apart from attending Sabbath services, my participation in each Session was minimal; however, I was deeply involved in the planning at world church headquarters.

After each Session—after the frenetic activity and celebrations faded—readers of the *Review* always asked the same question: Was it all worth it? I would give the stock, loyal reply: Yes! The Session cost a lot, but if you divide that figure among the world church membership, the amount is almost negligible.

That answer no longer convinces me. The flaw in the argument is that only a miniscule percentage of the membership—perhaps 1 percent—will ever have the opportunity to attend a General Conference Session. Only those fortunate enough to be able to pay their own way or to be selected as delegates or staff with all expenses paid can enjoy the experience. And those who attend at their own expense come overwhelmingly from America, Europe, and Australasia.

The numbers in Standish's editorial stick in my craw: $A30 million ($US24 million) and $A45 million ($US36 million). I have to face them now, not as *Review* editor but as a member in the pews. I have to tell you that I now view them as unconscionable. Unconscionable in terms of the gospel commission to take the story of Jesus to a dying world. Unconscionable in terms of hungry children and refugees and men and women without shelter—shivering, starving, dying.

And we—we who make a great profession of having "the truth"— we spend $36 million! For what—to give us feelings of pride? How will we face our Lord when He says: "Truly I tell you, whatever you did not do for one of the least of these, you did not do for me" (Matthew 25:45, NIV).

At this point in my life when perhaps I see more clearly what really matters and what is only fluff and window dressing, I can no longer give assent to the inordinate expense associated with holding General Conference Sessions like the San Antonio event.

And the actual expenses are far more than the estimates made by James Standish. The shocking fact is that no one—not the GC Treasurer, no one—really knows the total cost. Hundreds (thousands?) of people work ahead of a Session, during it, and following it. A huge amount of energy and time goes into making it the super-organized, jaw-dropping extravaganza that it has become.

An Adventist extravaganza. Adventism at our best. And also at our worst?

It wasn't always like this. For more than 100 years of our history, General Conference Sessions were small enough to be held in churches—as in the famous 1888 Session in Minneapolis, Minnesota, or in Sligo Church in Takoma Park, Maryland. But something happened over the course of the last 70 years. Independent ministries in a host of areas sprang up and multiplied. Today they number many hundreds. All seek a place in the Adventist sun; all seek to be seen and heard and to be able to explain their activities and make their pitch when Adventists gather together in large numbers—that is, at a General Conference Session.

Planning for GC Sessions never stops. As soon as one Session shuts down, the next one becomes the focus. Actually, planning has already been in place years before. So large has the Session become that very few venues on Planet Earth offer the facilities to meet its varied needs: seating for audiences of 70,000 or more on the two weekends, multiple rooms for committee breakouts, a huge area for exhibits by church and para-church ministries, accommodation for thousands of delegates and staff, as well as for many thousands of others who plan their dream vacation or trip of a lifetime in attending a General Conference Session.

The GC Session—Adventist extravaganza! Adventist version of an American political convention! So much energy! So much creativity! So much to blow you away!

But also—so much money. So much diversion from mission. Every fifth year in the Adventist cycle the work ratchets back into low gear as leaders prepare for the upcoming Session.

Isn't it time to rethink what we are doing and where we are headed?

And here is the irony: the current format, with all its work, glitz, and expense, no longer serves the purpose for which the General Conference Session was established. The GC Session is supposed to be a business meeting! But try to conduct business with more than 2,000 people "around the table"—impossible! The system has broken down, collapsed before our eyes. San Antonio was the tipping point. The pastor of the largest Adventist church in North America—the Loma Linda University church, with a membership of more than 6,000—arrived early on July 8 and lined up to speak to the issue of women's ordination scheduled for that day. He waited, and waited, and waited while time was frittered away on countless points of order. Waited and waited. Time ran out; he was never given opportunity to speak.

Is this my church? I can hardly believe it.

We need changes, big changes. Something has to give!

Here is my suggestion: It's too late to change the next General Conference Session (2020), but for 2025 let's convene, not in the United States, but in the global South. Make it way smaller, without all the add-ons. Cut the expense to $5 million total. Even that is a lot!

Time to Scale Back

It's time to begin thinking about reforming church structure at all levels. We need organization that is simple, small, and fair. Organization that is lean and lithe—focused on mission rather than on bureaucracy, on the local church rather than the top.

Let's start at the top. The General Conference grew over the years as the world church grew. When the "mission fields" were young and yet to develop national leaders, a headquarters staff that would nurture and guide them was necessary. Those days are long gone. The organization at headquarters in Silver Spring, Maryland, is way too big. It needs to be scaled back and replaced by a greatly reduced work force to serve the world field.

The employees of the church at headquarters work hard in the main, giving earnest, dedicated service. Their lives revolve around committees and travel; they constantly try to develop new programs that will "finish the work." When I was one of them, I found myself on some 40 committees—and others were on far more! The people there tend to find their identity in the number and importance of the committees of which they are members. Conversations typically deal with where have they just returned from and where they are headed next.

I don't wish to seem to put down these my former colleagues. They are fine people. It's just that from the pew, far removed from Silver Spring, all the committees and all the travel seem poles apart from the needs of suffering, desperate humanity.

We need to take stock and scale back. Unless we do, I'm afraid the course we are on will take us ever more toward a centralized, top heavy, Vatican-like organization.

What would a scaled-back General Conference look like? A much smaller operation. In one respect only would I add personnel: I think every division of the world church should be represented at the highest level to ensure fairness. And what of the many ministries and services? Cut, cut, cut to the bone. The present General Conference building will become too large for the reduced staff; headquarters can be relocated in a more modest facility.

Changes Are Coming!

I think it is inevitable that General Conference finances will tighten considerably. A major reason is that North America, which from the earliest days has been the financial foundation, will have fewer funds to send on upward to the General Conference. Two trends in the North American Division will be responsible for the change.

First, giving patterns are changing. Throughout our history the tithing principle has furnished a solid, steady base on which church finances have been built. But the generation that accounted for financial security is aging, passing off the scene. Those that come after it seem much less inclined to send a regular ten percent of income to support church organization. The millennial cohort in particular exhibits patterns of behavior that radically depart from those before them. Wary of organization in all areas of life, they tend not to be joiners. For example, their relation to the gym in large cities reverses that of their elders: instead of taking out membership in a fitness club, they prefer to hop from site to site, paying a one-time fee.

The church inevitably will be affected. These members don't feel the same loyalty to a local church congregation or to the larger Adventist church nationally and globally. When they return tithe—assuming that they do—they are more likely to decide for themselves where to send it instead of having the church decide on the distribution of the funds.

The upshot? Fewer funds flowing into the treasury on an assured basis. Hence, fewer funds sent on to the General Conference.

A second factor will magnify the shortfall: the needs of North America itself will demand that a larger piece of the financial pie stay right here.

The North American Division has attempted to face its future. It commissioned a major study that brought its findings in a large, candid report presented to the division year-end meeting. The report looked at structural reorganization, such as reducing the number of administrative units (union conferences and conferences). Radical restructuring could result in savings of some $150 million annually.

Loren Seibold, a church pastor for many years, with a keen analytical mind, has examined the status of small churches in the division. His sobering conclusion: within 10 years we can expect 1,000 small Adventist churches to disappear. They have no young people; they are dying. Across the division pastors are crying out for a larger share of the tithe to be retained for ministry at the local level.

The financial challenges extend to education: students in K-12 schools have declined sharply; several academies have closed; colleges and universities face increasing enrollment concerns. The problems are real, the numbers daunting. The conclusion seems inescapable: the North American Division will have fewer funds to send on to the General Conference treasury. Its own mission will demand that it retain more of the funds generated in its territory.

The General Conference needs to appoint a blue-ribbon committee to face the facts and explore contingencies. No option should be kept off the table. And the committee should include the best financial minds, from business and academia, as well as among church employees.

Big changes are coming. Will they be planned or unplanned? Will financial stress force them upon the church, or will leaders have the wisdom and courage to see and act before it is too late?

Anciently it was said of the men of Issachar that they "understood the times and knew what Israel should do" (1 Chronicles 12:32). May the Lord raise up such men and women for the Adventist church today!

CHAPTER
SIX

Adventists and Creation:
Jubilation or Confrontation?

The heavens declare the glory of God;
The skies proclaim the work of his hands.
—Psalm 19:1 (NIV)

I N THE BIBLE, BOTH OLD TESTAMENT and New Testament, the doctrine of Creation holds a high place. The God we worship, the God we serve, is Creator of heaven and earth; we are not God but creatures He has made. This belief is bedrock to the entire Scriptures.

The biblical response to this reality is joyful celebration. The angelic hosts burst into rapturous praises as they acknowledge the fact. Heaven's courts ring with joy; every creature in every realm—from the heights to the ocean's depths—joins in exultant praise and worship. That is how they react to the doctrine of Creation.

Do we?

A strange distortion has beguiled Seventh-day Adventists. We who more than most followers of Jesus emphasize Creation spend little time in jubilation. Instead, this basic teaching of the Word has become the nexus of argument, debate, polarization, and suspicion.

The San Antonio Session brought to the fore the passions stirred up by this topic as delegates disputed over the revisions of Fundamental Belief 6, Creation, that were brought to the Session. Eventually the changes recommended by the General Conference were voted with strong support, but it seems certain that the last word on this fundamental belief has not been spoken. Rather than resolving the problem, rather than removing the polarization, the new statement is likely to exacerbate the differences. Specifically, will Adventists enter a new era characterized by suspicion of science and scientists? And what about Adventist scientists: will they find themselves increasingly isolated in our colleges and universities?

Important issues are at stake. On one hand, those who pressed for changes in the wording that had been in place since 1980 did so out of a concern that this foundational biblical truth not be compromised. Those on the other hand were likewise concerned that the doctrine be retained true to its biblical expression without attempts to amplify or explain its meaning beyond the words of Scripture.

Behind the whole debate was the role of science in Adventist beliefs and practice. In San Antonio our church came face to face with basic questions that many other Christian bodies have been forced to address since Charles Darwin's *On the Origin of Species* burst upon the modern world in 1859.

While many Bible-believing churches have been convulsed by

the issues raised by evolutionary theory, the matter cuts with particular sharpness among Seventh-day Adventists. Our most distinctive practice—the observance of the seventh day of the week as the Sabbath—is at stake in the debate. But even more is on the line: not just the Sabbath but the Lord of the Sabbath, Jesus Christ.

Our longstanding approach to the natural world forbids us from retreating into an obscurantist stance that refuses to face squarely the challenges posed by scientific evidence. We hold that the Scriptures are God's revelation to humanity, inspired by the Holy Spirit, but we also believe that nature is God's second book, not as perfect as the Bible, but nonetheless important to teach us about God and His character.

Throughout our history Adventists have encouraged study of the natural world and have held in respect those who give their lives to that investigation. Our educational institutions include the study of science in the curricula at all levels, and in a variety of fields some Adventists have become leading researchers. In particular, we have fostered research in areas related to health, so that Loma Linda University Health has become internationally recognized for cutting-edge research.

For Adventists, therefore, the controversy between creation and evolutionary theory can never be reduced to an either-or acceptance or rejection of either the biblical data or the scientific. We believe that both have one Author. We are compelled to wrestle with the tensions that arise from both areas.

Thus one finds in our church an organization unique in the Christian world—the Geoscience Research Institute. This body, set up and funded from the highest levels of the world church, has as its mission the very wrestling described above. Its staff are all dedicated

Adventists and are all scientists with earned doctoral degrees from reputable universities. They endeavor to accomplish what a host of other scientists and a host of Christian believers have deemed impossible—the harmonization of the data from Scripture with the evidence from the natural world.

All this argumentation among Adventists is a far cry from the celebration of Creation that we find in the Scriptures. From jubilation to suspicion; from singing to fear of losing one's job; from rejoicing to uncertainty where the church is headed—how did we ever arrive at this point?

How We Got Here

Right from the outset of the Darwinian age, leaders of the Adventist church found it impossible to reconcile the evolutionary theory of the origins of life on earth with the biblical record of Creation. Ellen White wrote strongly against the new ideas, as did other pioneers of the young movement. Initially the Adventist response was based on biblical and theological arguments, but with the 20th century a series of Adventist apologists began to attack evolution on scientific grounds. Foremost among them was George McCready Price, whose writings catapulted Adventists to the forefront of those who continued to hold to the traditional, biblical view of Creation. Price was followed by Frank Marsh, Harold Coffin, and other creationist Adventist scientists. Thus, through most of the 20th century Adventists not only exposed Darwinism, they led the movement against it.

From Ellen White to McCready Price and his successors, Adventists were united in believing that the earth was young. They affirmed that the Creation accounts in Genesis 1-2 describe events that occurred in the recent past—some 6,000 years ago.

From the beginning of the debate with Darwin by conservative Christians, the 6,000 figure has been a watershed, a litmus test. For Adventists it assumed special weight because Ellen White referred to it numerous times in her writings, usually qualifying it with terms like "about 6,000 years" that in no manner weakened the force of the number.

That number, however, was not arrived at from specific biblical declaration. It originated with James Ussher, the 17th-century archbishop who pieced together the genealogical records in Scripture, added the numbers, and arrived at October 22, 4004 BC, 6 p.m. as the date of Creation. For many years copies of the KJV carried on each page dates based on Ussher's chronology.

Although some Christians, including Adventists, continue to hold to a strict, Ussher-based 6,000 figure, most who advocate a young earth time frame have moved to a more flexible understanding. Ussher's methodology was flawed: it failed to take account of the gaps in the biblical genealogical lists that a careful study reveals. Nevertheless, while setting aside a 6,000 number, young earth creationists think of less than 10,000 years, or at most less than 20,000 years.

Thus, the 6,000-year number, explicit or implicit, functioned and still functions as an anchor, a bulwark to safeguard a recent Creation and with it the Sabbath.

For some Adventists the 6,000-year banner has been important for reasons other than the doctrine of Creation. They have seen it pointing to the imminent return of Jesus. The reasoning is as follows: The Bible teaches that "with the Lord a day is like a thousand years, and a thousand years are like a day" (2 Peter 3:8, NIV), so if Creation took place around 4000 BC, then 2000 AD marks the beginning of the seventh 1,000-year period—the Millennium as prophesied in the

20th chapter of Revelation.

If one accepts the 4004 BC date from Ussher's chronology, the sixth 1,000-year day expired in 1996 AD. Not surprisingly, books written by Adventists announcing the soon return of Jesus based on this calculation circulated widely in the 1990s. The topic found eager listeners at camp meetings and in sermons as preachers used it to stir up the people. But 1996 came and went, as did the year 2000. The world entered a new millennium. And still the days pass by relentlessly. Understandably, the 6,000-year argument for eschatology has faded: it has been falsified by the passage of the years.

McCready Price was an educator, not a scientist. His attacks on evolutionary theory were based not on field observation but on the work of others. He powerfully laid bare the flaws in the arguments centered in the fossil record: the "gaps" in the sequence, the inability to account for the sudden appearance of new life forms, and so on. His successors (Clark, Marsh, et al.), however, were trained scientists. Likewise the staff of the Geoscience Research Institute. Those Adventist scientists look to the Flood as the explanation for much of the phenomena we find in nature today.

For the early Adventist defenders of Creation, the evidence for which they had to give account came from only one field—geology. Today, however, with the explosion of research, the task is many times more difficult. Now converging lines of investigation—from radiometric dating, plate techtonics, ice cores, and DNA, along with the geologic column—point seemingly inexorably to our planet's being infinitely older than 6,000 years. The accumulating data, rather than supporting a young earth, argue for the exact opposite.

How will Adventists relate to this data? Will we try to deny it? To bury our heads in the sand? Invent some theory of Satan's falsifying the natural data in an effort to deceive us?

One example: the dinosaurs. When the first dinosaur fossils were discovered, some creationists flatly denied their existence because such creatures didn't fit the grand scheme of Creation. Then more dinosaur bones were found, and more, in many different places and countries, until the evidence no longer could be denied.

Our Adventist heritage of openness to study of the natural world calls us to face the evidence, no matter how disturbing—and to try to construct a metanarrative (an overarching schema, a big picture) that will include it.

The Long Shadow of Galileo

Adventist scientists, like their colleagues, work under the long shadow of Galileo Galilei (1564-1642). In his writings Galileo presented evidence that the earth revolved around the sun, and not vice versa. It was an idea already advanced by Copernicus. But for the theologians of the church, who held, supposedly on the basis of the Bible, that the earth was the center of the universe, Galileo's teachings were heresy. Galileo was arrested and brought to trial in 1633. Faced with the threat of torture, he publicly recanted his views. His books were banned, and for the remainder of his life he remained under house arrest.

Arguments from Scripture trumped scientific investigation. It was a sad day for theology and theologians, as well as for biblical study.

Amazingly, only in very recent times—1992—Pope John Paul expressed regret at how the Galileo affair was handled and officially conceded that the earth was not stationary.

That year, 1633, the year of Galileo's trial and condemnation, was a tipping point in the history of ideas. Before it, theology trumped science; after it, science reigned over theology, radically changing the thinking and practices of believers and non-believers alike.

We Adventists place ourselves at great risk for our message and mission if we fail to heed the lessons of this sad chapter in Christian history. We must beware of pitting theology against scientific investigation. We must be rigidly faithful to the heritage derived from Ellen White herself—that Scripture and nature are both sources of truth, each shedding light on the other.

For Adventists during the 20th century, the doctrine of Creation, coming down with a young earth (read 6,000 years) understanding, became increasingly problematical. The data from the scientific world mounted to heights that forced reappraisal, while the dawn of the information age of TV, radio, and Internet spread the word everywhere. At the same time Adventist young people were seeking advanced degrees, in the sciences as well as in other disciplines; our colleges, once established primarily to supply personnel for the organized church, were offering majors, then masters, then doctorates in science as they increasingly morphed into universities. Among the youth, the majority attended public schools and were exposed to evolutionary theory.

Where was the Adventist Church headed? Some Church leaders became concerned that the doctrine of Creation—so important to us from the beginning, so vital for our Sabbath teaching—was threatened. The tide of naturalistic thinking that was washing over the world would, if unchecked, dilute our historic stance and eventually subvert it, as had happened with other denominations.

In this climate the 6,000-year number took on greatly added importance. Want a benchmark to gauge truth? Six thousand years. Want a line to draw in the sand, a line that shouted, "Not beyond this point!'"? Six thousand years.

Six thousand years. It was simple; it was uncompromising.

I recall a couple of incidents from the Theological Seminary at Andrews University, where I served as Professor of New Testament Exegeses and Theology and associate dean from 1975-1980.

The first incident occurred a few years before I arrived on the scene; it was still fresh in the minds of the Seminary faculty. The president of the university, under pressure from General Conference leaders, drew up a creedal statement to which all members of the faculty were expected to attach their signatures to indicate loyalty to orthodox Adventism. One point in the statement included belief in the 6,000-year period for the age of the earth.

The Seminary faculty was thrown into a quandary. For many the whole endeavor carried a bad odor. The problem wasn't that they didn't believe what they were asked to sign; rather, the process implied distrust and lack of openness. (I wasn't there, but I too have a problem with loyalty oaths anywhere, any time.)

The whole attempt failed, however. Perhaps it would have collapsed anyway, but it failed suddenly and totally when one faculty member declared that he could not support the 6,000-year dating with a clear conscience. That person was the revered Dr. Seigfried H. Horn, the father of Adventist archeology and the best-known Adventist scholar in circles outside the church.

Fast forward several years. I was now teaching at the Seminary, so I was a witness to, and participant in, what happened. Dr. Grady Smoot was now Andrews University president; Dr. Tom Blinco, dean of the Seminary; Elder Robert Pierson, president of the General Conference. Two vice presidents of the General Conference, Dr. Richard Hammill and Elder Willis Hackett, arrived on campus bearing statements developed at world church headquarters in Washington, DC. Elder Hackett was responsible for disseminating a statement on Inspiration and Revelation; Dr. Hammill was responsible for a second, on Creation and Age of the Earth.

I recall with fond nostalgia the dynamic that ensued. During the first meeting of the "Brethren" with the Seminary faculty, one professor, agitated and red-faced, denounced the statement on Inspiration and Revelation as "heresy" because he said it bordered on verbal inspiration.

The next day the group was enlarged to include religion and science teachers from the other schools of the university, as the focus shifted to the paper on Creation and Age of the Earth. Many of those present spoke; the meeting went back and forth, pro and con, for several hours. At last Elder Neal C. Wilson, father of the present General Conference President and at that time president of the North American Division of the church, rose to his feet. He had lived in Egypt too long, he said, and knew too much of that land's history and archeology to support the 6,000-year dating. You just can't fit in all the evidence. You need a longer time period.

Thud. The statement died at that moment.

That happened some 40 years ago. But the official worries about where we were headed as a church only increased. Making matters worse, reports of teachers promoting evolution in Adventist schools began to circulate. General Conference President Jan Paulsen took the initiative. He assigned Lowell Cooper, a general vice president, to organize conferences in every division of the world church to study the issues raised by scientific discoveries. Meetings convened at the national level and then internationally; the topic was thoroughly aired with divergent points of view openly expressed. The upshot was that the historic Adventist position was reaffirmed. Although it was not the consensus view, some of the attendees expressed strong support for a rewording of Fundamental Belief #6, Creation, to prevent any fudging on the time aspect—the age of the earth.

Which bring us to San Antonio.

Changes in San Antonio

For the first 120 years of our existence Seventh-day Adventists had no official statement of belief in Creation. In 1980, when the 27 Fundamental Beliefs were voted at the General Conference Session, a new statement was added, as follows:

> God is Creator of all things, and has revealed in Scripture the authentic account of His creative activity. In six days the Lord made "the heavens and the earth" and all living things upon the earth, and rested on the seventh day of that first week. Thus He established the Sabbath as a perpetual memorial of His completed creative work. The first man and woman were made in the image of God as the crowning work of Creation, given dominion over the world, and charged with responsibility to care for it. When the world was finished it was "very good," declaring the glory of God.

This statement, like the rest of the 27, was essentially an adoption of passages from the Bible.

Delegates to the San Antonio Session, however, adopted major changes, as a comparison of the previous statement with the new one reveals:

God has revealed in Scripture the authentic and historical account of His creative activity. He created the universe, and in a recent six-day creation the Lord made "the heavens and the earth, the sea, and all that is in them" and rested on the seventh day. Thus He established the Sabbath as a perpetual memorial of the work He performed and completed during six literal days that together with the Sabbath constituted the same unit of time that we call a week today. The first man and woman were made in the image of God as the crowning work of Creation, given dominion over the world, and charged with responsibility to care for it. When the world was finished it was "very good," declaring the glory of God.

The most obvious revision that confronts the reader is the new emphasis on the time aspect. Creation is now stated as being "recent," although no specific mention of a 6,000-year period is included. The "days" of Genesis 1 are stipulated as "literal days," while the Creation week itself is specified as "the same unit of time that we call a week today." All this in fact is encompassed in the opening sentence to which "and historical" is added to the previous "authentic account."

Those who worked on the revision obviously were at pains to modify the Creation statement in a manner that would preclude the possibility of understanding the "days" of Genesis 1 as long periods of time. In this they succeeded; however, two observations can be advanced.

First, the new statement is poles apart in mood from the biblical statements about Creation. In the Scriptures Creation evokes spontaneous doxology and adoration. The psalmist exults:

The heavens declare the glory of God;
the skies proclaim the work of his hands (Psalm 19:1, NIV).

Let all the earth fear the Lord;
let all the people of the world revere him.
For he spoke, and it came to be;
he commanded, and it stood firm (Psalm 33:8-9, NIV).

The New Testament takes the doctrine to even greater heights. We learn that it is the Word, eternal, equal to God, through whom "all things were made; without him nothing was made that has been made. In him was life, and that life was the light of all mankind" (John 1:3-4, NIV). And we find this glorious passage, possibly an early Christian hymn centered in Christ, who is Creator of all things in heaven and on earth:

The Son is the image of the invisible God, the firstborn over all creation. For in him all things were created: things in heaven and on earth, visible and invisible, whether thrones or powers or rulers or authorities; all things have been created through him and for him. He is before all things, and in him all things hold together. And he is the head of the body, the church; he is the beginning and the firstborn from among the dead, so that in everything he might have the supremacy. For God was pleased to have all his fullness dwell in him, and through him to reconcile to himself all things, whether things on earth or things in heaven, by making peace through his blood, shed on the cross (Colossians 1:15-20, NIV).

No wonder that the heavens resound in praise as every creature bows in adoration of the Creator:

You are worthy, our Lord and God,
    to receive glory and honor and power,
for you created all things,
    and by your will they were created
    and have their being (Revelation 4:11, NIV).

To bask in these passages and then return to the new fundamental belief on Creation is a huge letdown. On one hand we have worship, doxology, joy, rejoicing, adoration; on the other a prosaic statement that, intent on safeguarding Genesis 1 from misinterpretation, fails to portray the biblical witness to Christ the Creator.

We should also note that an important change in Adventist understanding of Creation is included in the revised statement. For the first time the concept of a two-stage Creation becomes official. A distinction is drawn between God's work of creating the universe and His activities in Genesis 1: "He created the universe, and in a recent six-day creation the Lord made 'the heavens and the earth, the sea, and all that is in them' and rested on the seventh day.'"

This teaching is at variance with that of the pioneers, including Ellen G. White. In their interpretation of Genesis they made no distinction between our world with its solar system and the rest of the universe. Here, for the first time in our official statement, the idea of a "gap" between the first two verses of Genesis 1 comes into play. God creates the universe but leaves our planet dark and lifeless for who knows how long? Perhaps thousands of years? Perhaps millions? Billions?

Implicit in this change in interpretation is acceptance of the geological data that suggest that our earth is very old. So now we have an old earth/young life view of Creation, with the Genesis account superimposed on the old earth theory.

Bulwark or Bogeyman?

The great majority of Seventh-day Adventists will neither be aware of the reworking of Fundamental Belief #6 nor concerned with the changes. For them, religion centers in the church that they attend each Sabbath. They hardly even know the names of leaders at the conference level and what transpires there, let alone developments at the other administrative levels of the church.

For others, the changes introduced in San Antonio will be welcome as a bulwark against a creeping evolutionism. Another group, probably smaller in number, will be troubled. They will see in the statement the potential for witch-hunting of science teachers (and possibly religion faculty) in Adventist colleges and universities. The new wording may become a bogeyman; ironically, the doctrine that deals with Creation will be used to stifle creativity.

If this happens, the 2015 General Conference Session will in time be recognized as a tipping point, when the Adventist church officially turned from its longstanding openness to God's revelation in the natural world to a path headed to obscurantism.

For church employees especially, the burning question will be: is this new wording to be considered descriptive or prescriptive? That is, does it describe Adventists' present understanding (at the official level), or is it a doctrine to which teachers and pastors must give assent? If the latter, we can see "sign on the dotted line or else!" scenarios quickly falling into place. They will bring searching times for faculty members whose conscience doesn't permit them to assent to something they cannot support, either because they read "recent" as indicating a period of time that the data deny, or because they are opposed to any approach that muzzles freedom to investigate and to explore new horizons.

I foresee a lot of arguing over what "recent" in Fundamental Belief #6 means. The General Conference President made it clear in discussion in San Antonio that for him "recent" signifies about 6,000 years. Others who believe in a young earth would go beyond the 6,000 years to 7,000 or up to 10,000. A diminishing number would be comfortable with 20,000 years; a few with 50,000. In light of the millions and billions of years that are bandied about in discussions of the age of the earth, even 50,000 years could be viewed as "recent."

I cannot resist a naughty thought as I contemplate such scenarios. What about the church employee who refuses to assent to the new wording because he or she does not accept the two-stage creation that has been introduced? Would such a person come under fire for holding to the position held by Ellen White and the pioneers?

I hope and pray that we as a people will avoid falling into the sort of scenarios that I have described above. The potential for disaster is there, however, and we need to be alert to it.

Beyond the issue of those employed by the church is the world of Adventist scientists. Today we can boast of many outstanding men and women, faithful church members, who spend their days (and nights) in a variety of scientific disciplines. Some work at leading research institutions, some have already made their mark among their peers. One is a Fellow of the Royal Society of Canada, and a Fellow of the European Academy of Sciences. In the United States, two Adventists are members of the prestigious Institute of Medicine National

Academy of Sciences.

For the most part these individuals have a low profile among us. But the day is not far off, I venture to suggest, when Adventists will be jolted to proud awareness because one of our number will be honored with a Nobel Prize.

We must affirm and encourage Adventist scientists, not be suspicious of them. And our statements of belief must be such that these brothers and sisters can support them without embarrassment.

The Conundrum

I believe that the Bible and the natural world alike testify of God, that both are sources of truth that we neglect at our peril. But how to fit together the pieces of the puzzle of our origin, our world, our history—that's the conundrum.

The world is wonderful; the world is horrible. Life—our life—is marvelous; life at times is almost too much to bear.

Jesus is wonderful. He, Creator of all things, lived and taught life, love, giving, unselfishness. In the world we find instead violence, predation, death. Within each of us—in our gut—are billions of life forms constantly being born, constantly dying.

Conundrum: who can solve it?

A thoroughgoing naturalism sees the universe as a closed system of cause and effect in which everything, including origins, is to be understood as wholly proceeding from natural causes. In this metanarrative, God is unnecessary and irrelevant. I reject this attempt to solve the conundrum of existence because it fails to take account of what to me is the primary datum—the reality of Jesus Christ and my life in Him.

So I am a supernaturalist: I believe in Creation. But I am also a realist; although I am not a scientist, I seek to be open to all the evidence, to take into consideration data that conflict, or appear to conflict, with the biblical metanarrative.

I do not have answers to the conundrum. Nor does anyone, I have concluded. Some answers, not all the answers.

The Bible, on which my life is built—the Bible through whom I became acquainted with Jesus, my Lord and Savior—supplies a hint at the answers. It tells us that evil is real, that a demonic entity opposed Christ long before our world began, and that this entity is responsible for the blight that has fallen over nature and our own lives.

Beyond this hint huge questions remain unanswered: How do Christ and Satan interact in the natural world? In what ways has Satan intervened in or manipulated natural processes? What new order—for it would be a new order—of existence would enable life without death in nature?

The quest to learn, to know, to understand goes on. And Adventists must be part of it, part of the answers to the conundrum.

CHAPTER SEVEN

Mission:
Beyond Counting Heads

*We talk of the Second Coming; half the world
has never heard of the first.*—Oswald J. Smith

A N OBJECTIVE OBSERVER OF THE ADVENTIST church might conclude that our favorite part of Scripture is the Book of Numbers. Of course it isn't, but we do have a fixation on counting heads.

Not all sorts of heads—just the heads of those newly baptized. We love it: so many baptized from this evangelistic campaign, plans for a large-scale effort with the goal of (drum roll) 100,000 new members, so many baptized in one day. A thousand, 3,000 (like the Day of Pentecost), 5,000 (now we are better than Pentecost). And so on and on.

The saints rejoice to hear about all the new members. Successful soul-winners become heroes. Some become the obvious choices to fill leadership positions.

But there is a downside. Pastors who have few accessions to report—or, most embarrassing, none at all—dread workers' meetings where administrators take public record. No wonder sometimes children age 10-12 feel pressure to hurry to the water.

This Adventist focus is not all bad. The Great Commission, words of the Risen Lord, sound the marching orders for followers of Jesus: Go, make disciples, baptize, teach (Matthew 28:19-20). We should not forget it or dilute it. And some pastors need to be prodded to get up from their armchair and share the good news.

This I believe: every gospel worker who prayerfully goes about his or her calling to ministry will find souls who are, as Ellen White put it, "looking wistfully to heaven" (*The Acts of the Apostles*, p. 109), ready to be gathered into the fold. I have encountered them in the most unexpected places. They are everywhere, waiting, hearts already changed by the Spirit, ready to take the next step along the path to life eternal.

Not all soils are fertile for the seed of the gospel. Some are hard and stony, some are shallow, some thick with weeds, as Jesus taught. It is unfair and untrue to reality to expect that all servants of the Lord will see their sincere efforts equally fruitful in the number of baptisms.

Nor are all baptisms equal. One minister's toil brings a harvest of only one person, and the minister may feel a failure. But the Lord doesn't count like we do. Every soul who chooses Jesus and the kingdom is of inestimable worth. And that one soul may, under the nurturing influence of the Spirit, become an H.M.S Richards or an Ellen White.

In 18th century London a troubled young man seeking peace with

God happened upon a religious service in Aldersgate Street. The speaker was a layman, unremarkable and unknown to subsequent generations. Led by the Spirit, he preached a simple gospel message. The young man felt his heart "strangely warmed"; his life was changed from that evening's encounter. John Wesley would go on to preach to many thousands. Joined by his brother Charles, he spearheaded a religious revival that transformed society.

Search through the Gospels and you fail to find warrant for the Adventist fixation on counting heads. Indeed, the Master Himself comes out poorly in terms of evangelism. All that preaching, but what meager results! Only 12 individuals stood by Him when the chips were down; one of them betrayed Him to His enemies, and another publicly denied that he even knew Him.

Was Jesus a failure? There's something wrong here—not with Jesus, but with the manner in which we Adventists have distorted the Great Commission. Jesus was faithful to His mission. He could declare at the end of His time on earth, "I have finished the work which You have given Me to do" (John 17:4, NKJV). He had brought the kingdom of God to earth and lit a flame that will never go out.

Think of the other great evangelist of the New Testament, the apostle Paul. He traversed the Roman Empire, planting churches in city after city. In some places the harvest of souls was bountiful, but elsewhere it was meager, by human reckoning. Paul never seemed to be concerned with counting heads. In some of the new churches, like Corinth, converts made a point of who was baptized by whom. But Paul dismissed all such talk as meaningless. He couldn't recall whom he had baptized: "For Christ did not send me to baptize, but to preach the gospel," he said (1 Corinthians 1:17, NIV). What a far cry from our obsession with numbers!

We have fallen into a worldly pattern of ministry. We have adopted a secular understanding of mission. Setting goals, counting heads, and measuring "success" belong in the boardroom, not in the church of God.

And here is the sad point: our head-counting is selective. We exult over the heads that go through the water, but we look away from the heads that walk or drift away from the church. We go to great effort and expense in public evangelism, but are we ready to find out how many of those who were baptized are still with us six months later? After a year? Two years?

Even a corporate model of mission would demand such an investigation.

It is high time for the Adventist church to change a lot of things in the way we go about fulfilling our God-given mission to the world. How did we ever fall into the un-Biblical pattern of reducing mission to counting heads? And where do we go—where should we go—from here? I am not a historian, but I have a theory concerning how it happened. My theory begins with a story involving my father.

One Hundred Forty-four Thousand and All That

My father was born in Sweden on one of the 30,000 islands of the Stockholm Archipelago. Leaving home at a young age, he sailed the world, first in sailing ships and then under steam power. He sailed down to Port Adelaide in Australia, fell in love with a brown-eyed local lass named Edith Painter, completed his contract, and migrated to the antipodes.

After a few years, now with children in the home, Dad made another big decision. One Sunday afternoon he went along to a park where anyone could stand up and hold forth on politics, religion, or whatever. That day Dad heard a man proclaiming the soon return of Jesus—an Adventist preacher. Dad became interested and then impressed; in due course he was baptized and joined the Seventh-day Adventist church.

All this happened a long time ago, at the time of World War I. There was considerable excitement among church members, he later related to me, because membership in the young denomination was approaching a number heavy with Biblical overtones—144,000. Today, the topic of the 144,000 (mentioned in Revelation 14) has faded from view, but back then it was hot. In the growing number of members, Adventists saw evidence of the soon End. Every new baptism brought it closer.

To us today such thinking seems incredibly parochial. The whole world, with its billions of men and women, and only 144,000 saved? Among all the churches and all the religions, only Adventists count? Amazing!

Well, the number count rolled along. It reached 144,000 and kept mounting. Jesus didn't come; that was a letdown. But the numbers game based on 144,000 continued. Had not Ellen White stated that not one person in 20 was ready to be translated? (She had.) So perhaps the critical mass was not 144,000 but 144,000 x 20. That mark was attained and passed. Jesus still didn't come.

Gradually interest in the question of who constituted the 144,000 waned. Interpretations built on the literal number slowly gave way to a symbolic understanding, as Revelation itself indicates (Revelation 7:9).

I cannot prove it, but I think it likely that the cryptic number 144,000 lies behind the Adventist penchant for counting heads. It has been and still is an impulse, a motivating factor, that is deep in the Adventist psyche.

On balance, I think our concern with numbers has served us more positively than negatively. Unfortunately, however, it has led us to view mission in a truncated manner that brought serious distortions.

It is time to rethink mission. What is our mission to the world? Let's begin by taking a look at what the Bible teaches about mission.

Mission in the New Testament

Readers of this book may be surprised at the preceding discussion. Some no doubt will respond that God has already given us our marching orders in the three angels' messages of Revelation 14:6-12. Along with them are the oft-quoted passages of the Great Commission (Matthew 28:18-20) and our Lord's words in Matthew 24:14: "And this gospel of the kingdom will be preached in the whole world as a testimony to all nations, and then the end will come" (NIV).

As important as Revelation 14:6-12 is in framing Adventist mission, we should look first to the Lord of the mission. How did Jesus, by His words and deeds, define mission?

For Jesus, mission centered in the kingdom, the *basilea*, the rule or reign of God. When Jesus began to preach, His message was: "The kingdom of heaven is at hand" (Matthew 4:17, KJV). The kingdom already was breaking through; heaven had come down in the person of God's Son. He was—is—the King of heaven; where He is, the kingdom is, as people yield themselves to Him as their Lord.

Thus, as Jesus commenced His famous Sermon on the Mount, He announced: "Blessed are the poor in spirit, for theirs is the kingdom of heaven" (Matthew 5:3, NIV). Not will be, but is. Even now the kingdom of heaven is here.

And the kingdom is not only in words, in preaching. It means new life; it means freedom; it means release; it means healing. Jesus' sermon delivered on a Sabbath in Nazareth made that clear. Quoting Isaiah 61:1-2, He declared:

> The Spirit of the Lord is on me,
> > because he has anointed me
> > to proclaim good news to the poor.
> He has sent me to proclaim freedom for the prisoners
> > and recovery of sight for the blind,
> to set the oppressed free,
> to proclaim the year of the Lord's favor (Luke 4:18-19, NIV).

In the tenth chapter of Matthew we find Jesus sending out the Twelve on a training mission. He "gave them authority to drive out impure spirits and to heal every disease and sickness" (v. 1, NIV), just as the Master did. As they went out preaching, their message was to be: "The kingdom of heaven has come near" (v. 7). They were to "heal the sick, raise the dead, cleanse those who have leprosy, drive out demons" (v. 8).

In Adventist mission understanding, Matthew 24:14 plays a key role. We view it, not merely as a call to all Christians in all ages, but as having particular application to ourselves because of our understanding of End-time events. We have tied together the coming of the End and the preaching to all the world in a relationship of conditionality: only when the gospel has gone to all the world will the End come. And so, when I joined the church as a teenager, we used to recite the aim of the Missionary Volunteer society: "The gospel to all the world in this generation."

The old MV Society, along with the Junior Missionary Volunteers, has ceased to exist, but the impetus derived from Matthew 24:14 continues, albeit in diminished form in much of the Adventist world. Many Adventists today are increasingly hesitant to make the *parousia* dependent on our proclamation of the gospel. They understand—correctly, I think—the text to simply state that when the Second Coming takes place the good news will have spread to the entire globe. It is a "sign" of the End, just like earthquakes, famines, plagues, and heavenly portents.

Setting aside issues of interpretation, however, this text so precious to Adventists continues an element that we overlook although it stares us in the face—"the gospel of the kingdom." Not just good news about Jesus, but the same message that He announced at the outset of His public ministry: "the kingdom of heaven is at hand" (Matthew 4:17, KJV). The kingdom—release, freedom, new life, healing, restoration. The kingdom—more than calling people to accept Jesus and be baptized.

Because the message we are to proclaim is the gospel of the kingdom, we can never reduce it to counting heads. To attempt to quantify it, to measure it by mapping countries as "entered" or "un-entered," is to truncate it in a manner that changes it.

The most succinct statement of Christian mission comes from the Risen Lord: "As the Father has sent me, I am sending you" (John 20:21, NIV). To carry on the work of Jesus—His healing, teaching, preaching—this is our mission. Not just His preaching, but His whole work.

In this regard Seventh-day Adventists shine bright in comparison with most other churches. Our emphasis on the whole person—spirit, soul, and body—and not just the spirit brings us much closer to the pattern set by our Lord than others who, perpetuating the ancient but unbiblical separation between body and soul, focus on preaching and teaching. To them a statement like Ellen White's "There is more religion in a loaf of good bread than many think" (*The Ministry of Healing*, p. 302) must seem incomprehensible.

Adventists not only teach wholeness, we practice it. We operate hospitals and clinics, prepare health foods, conduct seminars on wellness, help men and women find release from addictions, rush to bring relief when disasters strike, feed the hungry, and clothe the naked. We spend a huge amount of time and money in endeavors not directly related to proclaiming the gospel.

We have followed this multi-faceted ministry from the pioneer days of the movement. While we were yet young, with few members and fewer resources, Ellen White urged us to start a school, then a health care institution. As we began to grow in strength, as the cords of the Adventist tent stretched out wider, we added more schools, then colleges, then universities; and more clinics, hospitals, and medical schools.

Inevitably, tensions developed between the strictly ministerial (preaching) side of the work and the non-ministerial one. The conflict came to a head with the activities of the brilliant, mercurial Dr. John Harvey Kellogg, whose large center in Battle Creek, Michigan, became famous worldwide, attracting clients from leading figures in society and sports, right up to the President of the United States.

Ellen White saw no dichotomy between the preaching ministry and the medical ministry—both were aspects of the mission that Jesus Himself established. She went so far as to advocate that physicians be issued ministerial credentials, just like preachers. It was a radical theology, light years removed from the practices of other churches.

Unfortunately, a rupture developed as Kellogg rebuilt the Battle Creek San in grandiose fashion. A power struggle took place between the General Conference and Kellogg; it ended with the San passing out of denominational hands and Kellogg being removed from fellowship in the Seventh-day Adventist Church.

Losses on both sides were huge. The young Adventist movement was shaken to its foundations, but it survived and then flourished.

The schism left wounds that to this day are not fully healed. While both ministerial and medical wings have grown beyond anything the pioneers imagined, they largely have gone separate ways; the close relationship envisaged by Ellen White has been sundered.

From time to time church members and administrators voice doubts about Adventist hospitals. Staffed by nurses, doctors, and other personnel who aren't Adventists, with salary structures governed by prevailing market rates rather than denominational policy—are these institutions really Adventist? Are they worth all the effort they require from church administrators?

And here is the item of greatest concern to many—how many people are baptized after all this huge expenditure and effort?

All such talk is misguided. We aren't in the healthcare arena primarily to count heads. We do it because Jesus did it. He devoted most of His ministry to relieving human suffering.

It's high time to embrace wholeheartedly the medical ministry, along with the Adventist Development and Relief Agency and all activities that uplift humanity. To view them not grudgingly or as second-rate players but as full partners in mission.

To do so will radically reorient our understanding of mission. While evangelism will and should continue, we will break our fixation with counting heads and cease trying to measure "success" in the manner of a secular corporation.

These considerations lead us to notice in the Gospels something we often overlook—the difference between the kingdom of God and the church.

The Kingdom of God and the Church

In the New Testament we find a big difference between the Gospels and the other documents. In the Gospels "kingdom" occurs 102 times, sometimes as the "kingdom of God," sometimes as the "kingdom of heaven." (The expressions seem to be parallel.) Very rarely did Jesus refer to the *ecclesia*, the church. After the Gospels, however, "church" overwhelmingly predominates and "kingdom" almost disappears.

It is thus true to note, as others have before me, that Jesus preached the kingdom of God and the church was the result.

The church is not the kingdom of God. The kingdom embraces the church but encompasses far more.

The kingdom (Greek: *basileia*) is God's rule or reign. Wherever Jesus is confessed as Lord—wherever a person submits to His rule—there is His kingdom. The kingdom is invisible, silent. But real.

On the other hand, the church (Greek: *ecclesia*) is the community of the "called out" ones. It is visible, corporate.

The kingdom is wholly spiritual. It is unmixed, unalloyed. The church, however, is a mixture of the human and divine. Because it is a human institution, it is subject to the flaws and failings of humanity. It is not, cannot, be perfect on this earth. Leaders, no matter how dedicated, make mistakes. Inevitably political considerations come into play. At times in church history church leaders have fallen into gross abuses—arrogance, high-handedness, money grubbing, and corruption, including sexual immorality.

We Adventists have been around for only a comparatively short time, but, not surprisingly, the same sorts of abuses (although to a lesser degree) have manifested themselves. Even in Ellen White's time, now a century behind us, she sharply rebuked corruption at the highest levels of the Adventist church, especially the arrogation of "kingly power" at the General Conference.

It is devilishly easy to fall into the trap of persuading ourselves and others that, because we have been ordained to the ministry or have been elected by a committee to a post of leadership, we are endowed with special wisdom or have authority over our fellow church members.

We need to continually remind ourselves that the church isn't the kingdom of God, and heed the lessons of our history.

Another pitfall—and it's a big one—is thinking of the church as a corporation. For some years a major committee of the General Conference was the "Management by Objectives Committee." Looking back on it, I can scarcely believe that name. It represented a purely corporate model of the church, with goal setting, evaluations, and measuring "success."

How far from Jesus' commission: "As the Father sent me, I am sending you"! The church is a spiritual body, not General Motors or Ford. We must never permit worldly modes of thinking to influence our understanding and practice of mission.

Reflections on Mission

During our senior year at Avondale College, Noelene and I received a call to serve in India. This was remarkable on at least three counts: we had not yet graduated, we had not applied for overseas service, and we were not engaged—let alone married. The terms of the call and the duties we were to fill presupposed that we would be partners in the mission: I as dean of boys and a Bible teacher, No-elene as a music teacher at Vincent Hill School, a boarding academy at Mussoorie in Northern India.

We are profoundly grateful for our 15 years in India. The experience opened our eyes to the world, enriched us, broadened our horizons, and introduced us to wonderful students and colleagues whom we still count as friends. It launched us on a life trajectory—Australia to India to America to the world—that we could not have dreamed of.

We will be eternally grateful that when the call came, the Lord gave us the grace to answer, "Yes!"

Looking Ahead...

Mission is the lifeblood of the Seventh-day Adventist Church. Mission is woven into our identity; mission defines who we are and why we exist. When we abandon mission, we will die.

The issue, therefore, is not *whether* but *what*. What sort of mission will motivate us in the years ahead? Will we break the fixation with numbers, and understand and do mission in the spirit of Jesus, who came to make men and women whole?

CHAPTER EIGHT

Interpreting Scripture: Will Ellen Have the Last Word?

The writers of the Bible were God's penmen, not His pen.—Ellen White

I F THE WOMEN'S ISSUE DOMINATED ADVENTIST thinking during the period before the San Antonio General Conference Session, the five years following it will be focused on issues of interpreting the Bible.

Indeed, the sharp polarization over the role of women in large measure stemmed from different approaches to reading Scripture. Sincere Adventists on both sides coming to the same Word found themselves reaching differing conclusions. From the outset of our movement Adventists have been a "people of the Book," fiercely

Protestant in placing the Scriptures above priest and prelates, councils and tradition. "What does the Bible teach?" has been our watchword. But when the women's issue was studied closely, the teaching of Scripture didn't seem clear—certainly not to all. Some students argued that it supported, even mandated ordination of women; others concluded that it forbade the practice.

As those officially appointed to study the larger question of biblical interpretation take up their work in the days ahead, I have no intention of pre-empting the discussion. As someone who for many years has been a student and teacher of the Word, I simply wish to zero in on two areas that I think are crucial. The 2015 General Conference Session highlighted trends that have been developing over several years and that profoundly disturb me. The issues we are facing can be framed starkly as follows:

Will Adventists reverse course in biblical interpretation and veer in the direction of a literalistic/fundamentalist method?

Will Ellen White's writings become determinative in biblical study instead of fulfilling their time-honored function as a lesser light to illuminate the greater light, the Bible?

But first, a little history—how we have approached biblical interpretation during the relatively brief span of our existence—and then a brief personal account of my encounter with the Bible.

Adventists and the Bible

Adventists take the Bible seriously, have done so from the days of the pioneers and still do today. Without the Bible the Seventh-day Adventist Church wouldn't exist: it was study of the Word alone that led the pioneers of the movement to the two doctrinal planks enshrined in our name: the seventh-day Sabbath and the expectation of the soon return of Jesus Christ. We hold several other distinctive teachings, and all likewise became part of our belief system as the result of study of the Bible.

Many Christians likewise hold the Scriptures in high regard and profess to derive both doctrine and practice from them. We Adventists, however, differ from them in our view of the Bible in two important regards, quite apart from our distinctive doctrines.

First, we have a dynamic view of truth. We do not look to a creed out of the past, as do Lutherans with the Augsburg Confession or Presbyterians with the Westminster Confession. For us, truth is progressive. A verse beloved of the pioneers was 2 Peter 1:12: "For this reason I will not be negligent to remind you always of these things, though you know and are established in the present truth" (NKJV). Truth wasn't just truth; it was present truth.

Thus, the Statement of the Fundamental Beliefs of Seventh-day Adventists has a preamble that contrasts sharply with the creeds of other churches:

Seventh-day Adventists accept the Bible as their only creed and hold certain fundamental beliefs to be the teaching of the Holy Scriptures. These beliefs, as set forth constitute the church's understanding and expression of the teaching of Scripture. Revisions of these statements may be expected at a General Conference Session when the church is led by the Holy Spirit to a fuller understanding of Bible truth or finds better language in which to express the teachings of God's Holy Word.

Not surprisingly, the church took a long time articulating an official statement of doctrine. While several lists of doctrines were developed, only in 1980 were the Fundamental Beliefs voted by a General Conference Session. They numbered 27; in 2000 a 28th doctrine was added. At the San Antonio Session several fundamental beliefs underwent significant rewriting.

This dynamic understanding of truth has significant implications. It positions Adventists for the possibility of change—even major change—in beliefs and practice.

Second, unlike most fundamental Christians, we do not believe in verbal inspiration (dictation) of the Scriptures. We hold strongly to their inspiration, but in a dynamic interplay of the human and divine, so that it was the Bible writers rather than their words that were guided by the Holy Spirit.

For the Muslim, the Quran is 100 percent a copy of a heavenly prototype. Every word, in Arabic, was given by Allah.

But not for the Adventist with the Bible: the Bible is at once the Word of God and the word of man. As the Word of God, it is perfect for the purpose intended by God, which is to lead readers to Him and His salvation in the Son. As the word of man, it bears the marks of our common humanity: variations in writing style, occasional grammatical mistakes and inaccuracies.

Ellen White expressed the view succinctly:

> The Bible is written by inspired men, but it is not God's mode of thought and expression. It is that of humanity. God, as a writer, is not represented. Men will often say such an expression is not like God. But God has not put Himself in words, in logic, in rhetoric, on trial in the Bible. The writers of the Bible were God's penmen, not His pen. Look at the dif-

ferent writers.

It is not the words of the Bible that are inspired, but the men that were inspired. Inspiration acts not on the man's words or his expressions but on the man himself, who, under the influence of the Holy Ghost, is imbued with thoughts. But the words receive the impress of the individual mind. The divine mind is diffused. The divine mind and will is combined with the human mind and will; thus the utterances of the man are the word of God (*Selected Messages*, Book 1, p. 21).

Adventists have come a long way since William Miller. A farmer, Miller wasn't versed in Greek and Hebrew. He arrived at his distinctive interpretations of biblical prophecy by employing just two tools—the Scriptures and a concordance; his Bible was the King James Version. Miller checked biblical text by biblical text, letting the Scriptures interpret themselves.

His approach—which viewed the Bible as essentially uniform over the variety of its literature (history, poetry, wisdom, prophecy, apocalyptic, Gospels, letters) and the 1,500-year span between its earliest writings and last—was continued by the pioneers of the Advent movement. They became masters of the Word, experts in comparing text with text, invincible in debate with clergy of other denominations.

This method of studying the Bible, which we might call a "flat" approach or proof-texting since it focused on individual texts rather than passages or books, served us well. It brought untold blessings to faithful lovers of the Word who opened the Bible and simply took it as it read. (Some people, in a variant of the approach, had the practice of opening the Bible anywhere and placing a finger on a random text, hoping that the Lord would by this means provide help or guidance!) No doubt the "flat" method is still the preferred approach of most Adventists worldwide.

I followed this method for years in my personal devotions, preaching, and teaching. Looking back, I wonder how I could have missed the import of Ellen White's profound counsel, that the Bible's thoughts are inspired, not its words. The "flat" approach centers in words, not ideas. I don't wish to sound harsh—except on myself!—but that method is better suited to the Quran than to the Bible.

The Lord opened my eyes when, on furlough from India, I enrolled at the Seminary in Berrien Springs for graduate studies. During pursuit of an MA in systematic theology, I took courses in biblical exegeses—one course on First Corinthians, the other on the Book of Hebrews. In these courses we didn't flit around the Scriptures; we stayed with one book, engaging it in careful study, seeking to allow it to disclose its original meaning, listening to it rather than listening to our own ideas.

For a little while the approach, new to me, was disconcerting. Passages that I thought I understood, when investigated in the light of the Greek text and their context, in fact, meant something different. But soon I became enthusiastically absorbed: I realized that to take the Bible seriously—as I had wanted and taught—I must be true to it.

Unfortunately, not all the class members shared my appreciation. Almost all were ministerial students; several were already ordained. They became upset with the instructor because it seemed he had cut the ground out from texts they had employed in Sabbath sermons and evangelism. They fretted and fumed in class and eventually complained to the university president, Dr. Richard Hammill.

Hammill launched an investigation. As part of it he decided to enquire of some of the students. His procedure was criticized widely by those in the know, but I think Hammill was seeking information to exonerate the professor rather than to be used against him. One day I found myself in the president's office as he discussed Dr. Sakae Kubo. What classes had I taken from Dr. Kubo? What had he taught? Did I find the classes out of line?

Although I was at first surprised at the interview, as well as a bit uncomfortable, I quickly decided to share my perspective. I told Hammill that I thought Kubo was being wrongly accused, that he simply let the biblical text disclose its meaning, which I appreciated greatly, but that some students were upset because the exegesis didn't conform with their preconceived understandings of the meaning of the text.

I do not know who else Hammill called in for his investigation, but I do know the eventual outcome: Dr. Sakae Kubo, one of the church's finest biblical exegetes, was removed from the classroom and placed in charge of the Seminary library.

I will always be grateful for those classes from Kubo. Not only did they open my eyes, they fixed in me a determination to be true to the text, listening to what it says, and let the chips fall where they may. Later I earned a Bachelor of Divinity degree (equivalent to the M. Div. in the US) from London University and then a Ph.D. from Vanderbilt University, majoring in Biblical Studies. For my doctoral dissertation I decided to write on the Book of Hebrews. At its heart was a long chapter exegeting Hebrews 9-10, a critical passage for the Adventist doctrine of the Sanctuary. Hearing of my work, an Adventist colleague warned: "Hebrews! That's a dangerous book for Adventists to get into!" Another professor from my Andrews days feared: "Bill, will you still be an Adventist when you finish at Vanderbilt?"

While I appreciated the concerns expressed, I was also puzzled by them. If any book of the Bible is problematic for Adventists, shouldn't we dig deep into it rather than avoid it? And as it all turned out, my dissertation breezed through in an amazingly short time. It broke new ground and has been quoted extensively in subsequent studies of Hebrews.

My experience at Vanderbilt has been replicated by scores of other Adventists. Worldwide the number of Adventists who have earned Ph.D. or Th.D. degrees in the biblical disciplines—exegesis, language, theology, history, archeology—must be in the hundreds. Adventist scholars present papers at learned societies, publish articles in leading journals, contribute to landmark volumes of essays, etc.

How far have we come in 170 years!

Adventist Interpretation Today

Today we find wide differences among Adventists in hermeneutics (method of interpreting Scripture). Most members aren't even aware of these differences, or fail to understand why this is even something to be discussed. They simply come to the Bible and read it as it is, glossing over passages they don't understand.

But every time we begin to read the Bible we are involved in interpretation. The text comes to us out of the distant past and from cultures vastly different from ours. Inevitably, we have to interpret.

A simple example should suffice to make the point. Jesus said:

If your right eye causes you to sin, pluck it out and cast it from you; for it is more profitable for you that one of your members perish, than for your whole body to be cast into hell. And if your right hand causes you to sin, cut it off and cast it from you; for it is more profitable for you that one of your members perish, than for your whole body to be cast into hell (Matthew 5:29-30, NKJV).

What does one do with a passage like this? If we take it just as it reads, take it at face value, we should chop off offending members of our body. "But," you reply, "obviously Jesus didn't mean us to take these words literally." Obviously? What makes it obvious? It hasn't appeared obvious to some Christians. The scholar Origen (185-254) took Jesus' words just as they read and cut off a very private part of himself!

I don't think Jesus meant us to understand these words exactly as they read, just as many stipulations of the Mosaic code don't apply in our times. (Do we forbid women to attend church during their menstrual period? Why not? See Leviticus 15:19-29.)

I could multiply examples, but surely there's no need of further illustrations of the point. Whenever we engage the Scriptures we are involved in hermeneutics, even though we may not be aware of it.

Two Approaches

There is a sense in which every reader's hermeneutic is private to themselves, because each of us brings to the text our individuality and life experience. That said, I think we can divide Adventist interpretation into two broad and contrasting camps—the "flat," literalistic approach, and the nuanced approach. The former tends to deny the need to interpret, to go beyond the literal meaning of the text. The nuanced approach, on the other hand, comes to the text aware of the challenges to understanding caused by time, culture, type of literature, and so on.

A passage that has been much debated in the discussions concerning the role of women is 1 Timothy 3:2. In the KJV it reads: "A bishop then must be blameless, the husband of one wife, vigilant, sober, of good behaviour, given to hospitality, apt to teach."

Some of those opposing ordination of women have made much of the words "the husband of one wife," arguing that the text thereby limits ordination to men. A woman, they say, cannot be "the husband of one wife."

This is a case of literalism taken to absurd limits. That which proves too much proves nothing: if the interpretation were correct, Paul himself couldn't be ordained because he wasn't married! Nor should Adventists ordain single men, as we have in the past and occasionally still do.

What then does "the husband of one wife" mean? It cannot simply mean "married," because then the one wife would be superfluous. No, the point is that a bishop should have only one wife—he shouldn't be polygamous. As the *Seventh-day Adventist Bible Commentary* points out, "concubinage and polygamy were sociably acceptable" in the society of Paul's time (vol. 7, p. 298), but Paul called the Christian church to a higher standard.

The NIV rendering of 1 Timothy 3:2 captures Paul's intent: "Now the overseer must be above reproach, the husband of but one wife, temperate, self-controlled, respectable, hospitable, able to teach" (1984 edition).

That the argument based on a literalistic interpretation of 1 Timothy 3:2 should have gained traction among Adventists is disappointing. An even more distressing development was the introduction of "headship" theology—something not part of our history—to oppose women's ordination. This theology flies in the face of biblical teaching, as the paper prepared by the Seminary faculty showed convincingly. I find it disturbing that this study, reflecting the thinking of some of the best minds in the church, was pushed under the rug in San Antonio. (You can find this study online at andrews.edu/sem. Click on "Seminary Statements.")

So this is where Adventists stand today vis-à-vis hermeneutics: we are sharply divided. Large numbers of our members, no doubt the majority, and including some administrators right up to the General Conference level, follow a "flat" approach to understanding the Bible. Another group, not as large, believe whole-heartedly in the inspiration of the Scriptures but take a nuanced approach to interpretation. Instead of a wooden literalism, they look to the principles that Scripture itself reveals.

This was the pattern that our Lord showed us. In the Sermon on the Mount, He took six case studies from the Torah and went beyond a purely literal interpretation. With each example He said: "You have heard that it was said...but I tell you...." (Matthew 5:21, 27, 31, 33, 38, 43). Here the Lawgiver expounded the meaning of the Law. He intensified it, radicalized it, supplanted it.

Again, when a lawyer asked Jesus, "Teacher, which is the greatest commandment in the Law?" He didn't reply, "All the commandments are equal." Instead He answered, "'You shall love the Lord your God with all your heart, with all your soul, and with all your mind.' This is the first and great commandment. And the second is like it: 'You shall love your neighbor as yourself.' On these two commandments hang all the Law and the Prophets" (Matthew 22:37-40, NKJV).

We find a similar nuanced approach to Scripture in Jesus' denunciation of the scribes and Pharisees. They were scrupulous in tithing garden herbs—mint, dill, and cumin—He said, but neglected "the more important matters of the law—justice, mercy and faithfulness" (Matthew 23:23, NIV). This statement echoes the great passage in Micah 6:8 that is the summit of Old Testament religion:

> He has shown you, O man, what is good;
> And what does the Lord require of you
> But to do justly,
> To love mercy,
> And to walk humbly with your God?

For some believers, every teaching of the Word has equal weight, and every rule for life from the Lord carries the same weight. But not for Jesus. He taught—and lived—that love of God is the supreme value, with love of neighbor a close second, and that justice, mercy, and faithfulness are the guiding principles of the lives of His followers.

The case studies above presuppose the most important principle of all in hermeneutics—Jesus' life and teachings are the touchstone. He is the Truth.

In this light we understand the meaning of His cryptic words: "If your right eye causes you to stumble, gouge it out and throw it away" (and the other sayings in the same vein in the Sermon on the Mount). Jesus proclaimed Himself as healer, liberator, restorer, and His entire ministry corresponded to His words. He didn't maim; He made the maimed whole. He didn't gouge out eyes; He made blind people see. Therefore His followers aren't to be in the business of maiming or blinding—quite the opposite. Jesus was about wholeness, ours and others', and so must we be. His sayings about maiming and blinding cannot be understood literally; they must be seen in the "kingdom" sense—meaning that any practice or habit that injures another has no place in the life of the citizen of the kingdom of heaven.

It also becomes clear that the hierarchical thinking that forms the basis of the "headship" theology is contrary to the life and words of the One who said, "Whoever wants to become great among you must be your servant, and whoever wants to be first must be slave of all. For even the Son of Man did not come to be served, but to serve, and to give his life as a ransom for many" (Mark 10:43-45, NIV).

Where are Adventist headed in interpreting the Bible—in the direction of a flat literalism or toward a nuanced hermeneutic that looks to Jesus for the last word?

Let me now briefly share my thoughts on a topic that, although separate from interpretation of the Bible, bears upon it: the use (and misuse) of Ellen White's writings.

Ellen and Scripture

I never had hang-ups about Ellen White. I discovered her for myself, and she showed me Jesus. I wasn't brought up in a home where I kept hearing, "Mrs. White says you shouldn't..." "Mrs. White says you should..." The red books were there in the home, lined up in the bookcase that stood in the hallway. Dad would get them out and read them. I saw him reading them, but he never turned them on me.

Maybe he did with the older kids. I don't know. I was the youngest and Mother hadn't become an Adventist. By the time I came along the wars over religion had all been fought and a truce declared. Under the terms of the peace, religion would be the one subject ruled out of discussion.

So Dad went to church and taught his Sabbath school class. He studied his Bible and read the *Signs of the Times*. He said the grace at meals, which always went: "For what we are about to receive may the Lord make us truly thankful. Amen." And he brought out Ellen White's books and read them to himself.

When I was around age 11, Dad encouraged me to start reading the Bible. Just to read, cover to cover, Genesis to Revelation. Then to read it again. And again. And again.

It was the best habit I ever formed. It has stayed with me for life. It has been, probably, the most important influence in my life. No matter why a person starts reading the Bible, if he or she keeps reading, the Bible will bring new life, new creation. That happened to me.

I began to talk to Dad about the Bible. I began to ask him questions. I wanted to know what "Selah" meant in the Psalms.

Dad knew the Bible and the Lord of the Bible. Step by step he nurtured the new creation. I wonder, now, how much prayer also went into that new life. I had become a Christian, born again, praying, believing, feeding on the Word—not attending church, not baptized, but a Christian.

Enter Ellen. I don't recall how I got started on her writings. If Dad introduced her—and I expect he did—it was so gentle, so low-key, that the incident didn't register. Ellen's writings did. I read myself through her works, and they showed me Jesus. *Steps to Christ* led me to forgiveness. *The Desire of Ages* helped me fall in love with the story of Jesus. *Christ's Object Lessons* opened up His teachings. *Patriarchs and Prophets* opened up the Old Testament, revealing Jesus. *The Great Controversy* introduced the last events leading to His return.

Ellen was never a club or a killjoy to me. I can understand—grasp mentally—how some people brought up on Ellen White have grown up hating her. I can understand, but I cannot enter that experience. And my advice to those people, like my advice to those people wanting to know about Adventists and what we think of Ellen, is: Read her. Read *Steps to Christ.* Read *Desire of Ages.* Read *Christ's Object Lessons.* Read *Patriarchs and Prophets.* Read *The Great Controversy.*

The Adventist Church still has a long way to go in coming to terms with Ellen. Our pioneers had a struggle, and the struggle goes on. Some in her day wanted no part of her counsel, just like today. Some in her day wanted to raise her writings to a level equal with Scripture, searching her words to explain Scripture rather than searching Scripture itself, just like today.

I suppose there always will be a continuum. Some Adventists will tend toward the pole of equating her writings with Scripture; others to the pole of limiting their value to her own time. We need to learn to live with these differences of perspective, to accept each other with these differences just as she learned and accepted them in her day. I wish we could set up boundary markers and keep hammering them in:

Boundary marker 1: Ellen's writings are not Scripture, are never to be equated with Scripture, but are always tested by Scripture.

Boundary marker 2: Her writings are inspired, of continuing value to the church.

I think these markers could be of enormous help in clarifying the role of Ellen to the world and to ourselves.

In recent years there seems to be a move to elevate Ellen's writings to a place equal to Scripture or even above it. The "lesser light" is becoming the "equal light" or the "greater light."

Am I wrong? I hope so.

When I read articles in church publications that are based more on her writings than the Bible, I cringe. When I hear sermons that look to her counsel rather than to the Scriptures, I ask myself, "What is going on?"

For many years I was involved in official dialogues between the Adventist Church and other denominations, first as a member of the Adventist team, later as its leader. When we began these dialogues, we encountered considerable suspicion and distancing: Are Adventists truly Christian or are they a cult? We appealed to our official statements that place us squarely in the Protestant, evangelical way of Christianity. Gradually we were accepted; eventually even the World Evangelical Alliance recognized us as a partner in fellowship with them (not a member; we did not seek to be organically joined).

Seeing and hearing some of the stuff Adventists are putting out today, I wonder how those leaders of other faith communions, who believed us when we said that for us the Scriptures are the preeminent authority, would feel? Deceived? I am troubled.

Then there's the growing practice among us of always having to insert several Ellen White quotations in an article or sermon, even when they don't add anything new, just to show that we're true-blue Adventists. Who do we think we're fooling by such religious games? We may impress our fellow believers, but not the Lord.

Some of the presentations in San Antonio alarmed me. Where are we headed? Have we reached a tipping point?

Contrary to her own counsel, is Ellen White to have the last word in interpretation?

CHAPTER NINE

The Promise of Adventism

AT ITS BEST ADVENTISM IS WONDERFUL. At its best it is a creative remnant, a leavening force in society.

Of course, Adventists aren't the only children of God. The Lord is a big God, too big to be put in a box and tied with a ribbon. God has many children just as He always has had, as He had in the days of the chosen nation. God works in multiple ways through a variety of agents.

In His grace He chose Adventists to play a part in His plan. Although like Israel we have oft-times been narrow-minded, exclusive, and narcissistic, when we have let God be God in and among us, the results have been superb.

Think of it: a small people with few resources believes in health and healing as part of the gospel, long before "wholeness" became a buzz word. This people develops state-of-the-art medicine, pioneers vegetarian foods when meat is the accepted diet, changes the breakfast habits of a nation. The same small people stand up for religious liberty for all people. They spread across the face of the globe; they build medical launches for the Amazon and unlock the nutrition in the soybean; they pioneer heart transplants for babies doomed at birth; they go everywhere and leave in their wake clinics, schools, hospitals.

There is much to be proud of in this history, even if that history has chapters of regret and shame. Adventism has been a movement of promise.

It can be again.

Adventist Hero

Adventism has had its heroes. It still does. I'll tell you about one.

Gillian Seton, eight years out of medical school, completed her five-year surgery residency at the University of Utah and accepted an assignment to work at Cooper Adventist Hospital in Monrovia, Liberia. Dr. Richard Hart, president of Loma Linda University Health, continues her story:

"She arrived in February 2014 and rapidly settled into a busy practice as the primary doctor at this small 25-bed hospital. As the summer of 2014 came on, rumors, the reports, started surfacing of Ebola infections from the countryside in Guinea, Sierra Leone, and Liberia. The latter two countries had recently emerged from long and bloody civil wars, with much of their civil infrastructure still fractured. There was hardly a worse place to deal with what soon became a major epidemic with global significance.

"As the infectivity and virulence of the Ebola virus became more evident, panic gripped the capital city of Monrovia. Those trying to care for these patients, both in the hospitals and at home, became infected themselves, with a high mortality rate. Soon the hospitals in the city started closing as workers became afraid to come to work or were consumed with caring for their own families. Our small staff at Cooper was exposed to the same concerns and fears, but determined to carry on. Finally, they were the only hospital caring for medical emergencies in this city of over one million, trying to assess patients in the parking lot to protect the staff and other hospitalized patents from Ebola. After several risky exposures despite all precautions, Gillian was offered a ticket home to protect herself. She refused, calmly stating, When there is a need, you do what needs to be done. Over the next year, through multiple exposures, forced temporary closures and evacuations, she returned again and again to care for those in need.

"Our School of Medicine senior class asked Gillian to be their speaker for commencement. Her message was short and powerful. She told of the challenges she faced personally and professionally as she watched a nation struggle and patients die despite her best care. She ended with three simple words of advice for our graduates. First, you are HUMAN. You will make mistakes and can't do it all. Accept that, don't let it defeat you. Second, you are not ALONE. Reach out to those around you, seek help, and reach up to our God for assistance. Finally, be BRAVE. It is amazing what the human spirit can accomplish when pushed to is limits. Our students thanked Gillian with a standing ovation."

Adventism at its best is wonderful, heroic. It has within it the power of promise.

The No-Baloney Jesus

Just before starting work on this book I completed a project on Jesus. I've written a lot of books that touch on Jesus, but never one that was just about Him, all about Him. For a couple of years I buried myself in the Gospels—Matthew, Mark, Luke, and John. Yes, I did consult some other books, including Ellen's classic *The Desire of Ages*, but not many. Overwhelmingly I stayed with the four Gospels, going through them one by one, reading them whole, then comparing each with the other.

I was blessed. It was wonderful. And yet it was difficult. I understand why almost everyone who sets out to write about Jesus sticks mainly with one Gospel—Jesus in Matthew, or in Mark, or in Luke, or in John. Four Gospels—they are marvelous, but they're puzzling. They tell you so much about Jesus, but they leave you with so many questions. The problem: they agree, but they disagree. They disagree not just in little matters but also in big ones. If you read Matthew, Mark, and Luke, you find a Jesus who is out-and-out a Galilean. He lives and preaches in Galilee and becomes immensely popular. But the religious Establishment gets upset and plots to kill Him. He goes up to Jerusalem for the festival of Passover, and there they arrest Him, put Him through a phony trial, and crucify Him.

But then you turn to John's Gospel, and everything changes. Jesus works in Galilee, yes, but also in Judea. He doesn't go up to Jerusalem just once for the Passover, but at least three or four times.

The writing came fast—amazingly fast. I tried to be honest with the text, to let Jesus step out from its pages, Jesus as He was, a first-century Jew, a poor man, an altogether unremarkable man—but the greatest man in the history of the world.

Not a "meek and mild" person. No way! Not a comfortable, feel-good fellow. Not on your life! The Jesus of the Gospels was—is—radical. He upset the tables of the money changers in the Temple, and He upset ways of thinking, ways of doing religion.

He upset the religious order—the theologians and the priests and the whole Temple system. He upset the civil authorities, who saw Him as a threat.

He still upsets the world.

He upsets the Adventist church.

He upsets me.

If you take Jesus seriously, He'll upset you.

He's the no-baloney Jesus.

The church is a great place to find baloney—religious baloney. Baloney loves organized religion. The dictionary defines baloney as "pretentious nonsense." The word can be used to dismiss an idea that's simply way-out, plain crazy, but often it carries a religious dimension. It signifies making a show of being good or pious but not living up to what you tell others they ought to do. Organized religion is full of it. And we Adventists have developed our own variety. We specialize in Adventist baloney.

What impresses me about Jesus of Nazareth is there's no baloney. He's real. He's authentic. What He preaches, He lives. He walks the talk.

He's the NO-BALONEY Jesus.

Jesus said a lot about religious baloney, but strangely, you won't hear that in our sermons. Maybe not so strange—His words about baloney cut too close to the bone for our comfort.

Jesus—no baloney.

The No-Baloney Church

Adventism without baloney: that's what I'd like to see in our church.

This little book, which may contain some stingers, is really a call for us—individually and corporately—to come close to Jesus.

It's a call for Adventism at its best—wonderful, heroic, authentic.

That "best," in my understanding of the Bible, is:

—people who build bridges, not walls. Who ensure that everyone has a place at the table—black and white, poor and rich, women and men, illiterate and educated;

—people who include, not exclude; who are light and leaven in society;

—people who live in joyful, confident expectation of Jesus' return;

—people who uplift Christ and His Cross;

—people who are authentic and real, who seek to carry on the ministry of Jesus without pride or pretentiousness;

—people who work to make men and women whole;

—people who love the Word and interpret it through the life and teachings of the Word made flesh.

This is the promise of Adventism: a ministry of hope and healing.

Walk Away? Never

In these strange times, these days of doubt, many are walking away from the church. I am not. Although the church at times makes you feel like you've been punched in the gut, the church is my home. Where would I go?

Much of what I am I owe to the Seventh-day Adventist Church.

Although it is feeble and defective—as, I think, the Christian church has ever been—it is my spiritual home. Where I belong.

I feel incredibly privileged. Since I accepted Jesus as Savior and Lord at age 16 and threw in my lot with the Adventist church, I have been immensely blessed. Not financially privileged—no silver spoon in the mouth—but privileged in ways immeasurably richer than dollars or euros:

Privileged to serve Jesus in India, a fabulous land of warm-hearted, gracious people.

Privileged to be given time to study the Bible at a deep level and to share the life and teachings of Jesus.

Privileged to guide the official paper for the church, and to lead in the development of a new one for the world body.

Privileged to sit on councils of the church with voice and vote.

Privileged to serve as a life trustee on the Board of the Ellen G. White Estate.

Privileged to travel the world, an ambassador representing the President of the church to other Christian leaders and to leaders of world religions.

So privileged! So blessed! And, now in retirement, still privileged:

Privileged to teach bright, eager young minds preparing for service in the healing arts, at Loma Linda University.

Privileged to become acquainted with the team of earnest men and women who, through The One Project, seek to make Jesus first and last and best in everything.

Walk away? I would be the worst of ingrates.

Adventism is a movement of promise. It fulfilled that promise to me.

The Edge

I have been blessed with excellent health. Completed 17 marathon runs. Climbed Kilimanjaro. Hardly missed a day in more than 50 years of work.

Numbers to be proud of: heart rate 42, blood pressure 120/65, cholesterol excellent. My heart, I used to brag, as strong as an ox.

Famous last words! In 2014, while on a visit to Australia, my world collapsed. Heart attack. Ambulance, sirens, lights, careening down the wrong side of the city streets.

Straight into surgery. Stent. Six days in a hospital ward.

My wonderful heart, strong as an ox, was diseased with multiple artery problems. At last, back in the United States, bypass surgery—for four blockages.

I was recovering slowly when suddenly the wheels came off. Complications from the surgery caused vomiting and a drastic loss of appetite. I landed back in the hospital. For weeks I walked the Edge; nauseated day and night.

For the first time in my life I could not pray. I didn't ever feel angry with God, but just too weak, too rotten to cry out for help.

I made my bed in hell. But even there I found Jesus. When I couldn't pray, I knew that Jesus was doing what I couldn't—He was praying for me. Even in the valley of the shadow, Jesus was there.

Slowly, slowly He brought me back from the Edge. Slowly I began to eat again. Slowly I began to wake up and thank God for the light.

That year, 2014, was my *annus horribilis*—the terrible year. For a long time I didn't want to talk about it, didn't want to think about it.

Then about six months ago, Noelene and I were sitting in our favorite restaurant when the thought struck me like a bolt: You should be grateful to God for your *annus horribilis*. What? Thank Him for that absolutely rotten year?

Yes, yes, yes! Think of what God gave you through that year!

So many things—so very personal that I find it difficult to put them into words.

First, I'm not afraid to die now. I've been to the Edge. I've looked over the Edge into the Abyss. And, my friends, it's not so bad. Jesus is there. He's there even when you feel so weak, so terrible that you can't utter a word.

Second, I can see clearly now; the rain is gone. So many things that used to bother me, that made me impatient—they don't amount to a hill of beans. All that small stuff I used to sweat—it's nothing, nothing at all.

Only one thing matters. Only one Person matters—Jesus.

Jesus, only Jesus.

The church is important, but when you've been to the Edge, all that matters is Jesus.

Doctrines are important, but they fall away when you've been to the Edge. There's only one Doctrine that matters—Jesus.

So now, my friends, I can say, "Thank You, Father, for my *annus horribilis*," and mean it.

In a strange new way I feel liberated. I'm a sensitive person and have always been concerned (too concerned!) about what others think and say about me.

I'm still sensitive, but I've been liberated. When you've been to the Edge, you come away knowing that the only One whose approval means anything is Jesus.

Someone doesn't like what I preach? Sorry, but if I spoke what Jesus put in my heart, that's all that matters.

Someone objects to something I wrote? That's OK, but I write only after consulting with my Lord, and He's the One I want to honor.

I thank God for the Edge!

I thank God for Jesus, Lord of the Edge!

Jesus, only Jesus, is all I need, all I desire now and forever.

Recently I came across a marvelous statement by Ellen White: "You will come up from the grave without anything, but if you have Jesus you will have everything. He is all that you will require to stand the test of the day of God, and is not this enough for you?" (Ms 20, 1894).

Jesus—He's enough for me.

Jesus is my Enough.

Now.

Forever.

CHAPTER TEN

Unity:
Top Down or Bottom Up?

I in them and you in me. May they be brought to complete
unity to let the world know that you sent me and have
loved them even as you have loved me.
—John 17:23

A
S EDITOR OF THE *ADVENTIST REVIEW* I worked directly under three General Conference presidents. My bosses,
to whom I reported, were in turn Neal C. Wilson, Robert S.
Folkenberg, and Jan Paulsen. I became closely acquainted with each,
spending many hours all told, not only discussing the activities of
the church paper but also developments and concerns of the church.

I can tell you that for all three presidents the overriding goal was
the preservation of the worldwide Seventh-day Adventist Church. We

are such a diverse, scattered fellowship, a marvelous conglomeration from "every nation, and kindred, and tongue, and people" (Revelation 14:6). How to keep the family—this family drawn from more than 200 nations—together? That is the huge challenge.

We have been around for more than 140 years now, and we are still together. It is the Lord's doing, and His alone. We have grown and spread, but still we are together. In a manner that Christians of other churches can scarcely grasp, we are knit together by ties of love and appreciation. You can step off a plane in Bombay or Buenos Aires, London or Lagos and meet people totally new to you—but Adventists—and at once you feel safe, at home with them.

This union is precious, but it is fragile. May we never do anything to put it at risk.

Although our members now total about 20 million, we have come this far without a major split. Twice during our history the skies loomed dark with impending disaster, but the Lord brought us safely through the storm.

The first crisis of unity came at the beginning of the 20th century. At its center was the brilliant, famous, mercurial doctor, John Harvey Kellogg. He had built up around himself a mini-empire with the Battle Creek Sanitarium its masterpiece; he commanded a following larger than that of the General Conference under the leadership of Arthur G. Daniells. Kellogg had some deviant ideas, but the issue at stake was control—control over the medical ministry and outreach of the church. The struggle was fierce, the outcome for a while uncertain. In the end Kellogg went his own way, taking with him the beloved San and a large number of supporters. The church, diminished, struggled on, recovered, and forged ahead. Kellogg's dreams crashed in the 1930s when the San defaulted and passed out of his hands.

The second major threat to unity arose in Germany during the First World War. Leaders of our church, caught up in the nationalistic fervor aroused by Kaiser Wilhelm, compromised Adventist principles of non-involvement with the state. The church split; members who could not abide the actions of their leaders broke away to form the Reformed Seventh-day Adventist Church. It continues to this day, but is very small, numbering a total of about 35,000 worldwide, while the official Adventist church adds more than one million new members every year.

Today, however, ominous developments threaten to fracture our precious unity. Many voices are expressing deep concern. On October 4, 2016, Norwegian Union Conference leaders, in a statement released on the union's website, warned, "Never before in the history of the Seventh-day Adventist Church have we been closer to a major split of the church."

Whatever led these Norwegian administrators to such a conclusion? Very recent developments that came to a head at the 2016 Annual Council.

A Momentous Council

Although I do not try to stay tuned to developments at world headquarters of the church—I had my day and now am content to sit back and let others handle the work—for some time I had been hearing disquieting rumors. They suggested that leading officers of the world church were planning to take action against the "disobedient" union conferences, those that continued to ordain women pastors. Although several union conferences in Europe have voted steps aimed at putting men and women ministers on the same level—such as having commissioning for all, or none at all—the General Conference leaders had as targets two union conferences in the North American Division: the Columbia Union in the east and the Pacific Union in the west.

That the continuing activities of these two unions caused displeasure to some at church headquarters did not surprise me. What I began to hear, however, seemed so unthinkable that I refused to take it seriously. It was rumored that the General Conference was contemplating disbanding the leadership of these unions and bringing them directly under General Conference control. The General Conference would then work to have new leadership put in place, leadership that would reverse the previous voted actions of the union committees that had authorized ordination of women.

I did not want to believe such talk; it belonged to some other world, a nightmare world, not the General Conference where I had served for 26 years.

I was wrong. The 2016 Annual Council showed that the rumors were not crazy: General Conference leaders had determined to bring the Pacific and Columbia Unions into line by threatening the "nuclear option"—taking over the unions.

I was appalled. I am still appalled. I have lost many hours of sleep over the dire outcomes of such an ill-advised plan. I think the grave conclusion of our leaders in Norway is correct.

Throughout the course of my ministry, which covers nearly 60 years, I have been supportive of leadership. I take seriously the biblical injunction: "Remember those who rule over you, who have spoken the word of God to you.... Obey those who rule over you, and be submissive, for they watch out for your souls, as those who must give account" (Hebrews 13:7, 17, NKJV). Now I find myself in the unaccustomed role of calling them to account. I would prefer to stay quiet, to keep my deep concerns to myself, but I cannot. One day, perhaps soon, I shall stand before the Lord and give account for my words—or lack thereof. On that day it won't be a matter of whether someone at the General Conference or anywhere else is upset by what I wrote. Jesus, only Jesus—He is my Boss.

Why am I appalled? Because the course of action that the General Conference leaders contemplate—and we can know it now not by rumor but by their own documents—is wrong. Wrong from any angle you look at it. Wrong in its theology. Wrong in its history. Wrong in its policy. Wrong in its spirit. It is more papal than Seventh-day Adventist. It runs directly counter to the life and teachings of Jesus, who taught us: "You know that those who are regarded as rulers of the Gentiles lord it over them, and their high officials exercise authority over them. Not so with you. Instead, whoever wants to become great among you must be your servant, and whoever wants to be first must be slave of all. For even the Son of Man did not come to be served, but to serve, and to give his life as a ransom for many" (Mark 10:42-45, NIV).

Strong words! Let me share why I reached this conclusion. I will cut to the chase, zeroing in on the principal issues involved. They boil down to three: the ordination of women clergy, the role of union conferences, and the authority of the General Conference.

Ordination of Women—Facts and Fiction

For some Adventists who oppose ordination of women clergy, the course proposed by the General Conference makes sense. Some might argue that the leaders should take such action and without delay, because the non-compliant unions are in "rebellion." The reasoning is straightforward: Three General Conference Sessions (1990 in Indianapolis, 1995 in Utrecht, and 2015 in San Antonio) voted against women's ordination. The actions of the General Conference Sessions represent the will of God; therefore, those who refuse to abide by the decision of the Session are demonstrating their opposition to God's will.

Simple? Not so simple.

Here are the facts relative to women's ordination:

First, ordination of women has never been forbidden by a General Conference Session. The major discussions on this topic took place during the 1990 Session, when a long, full discussion took place, extending over two days so that everyone who desired to speak could be heard from. The action taken did not express disapproval of women's ordination, but it noted the lack of a consensus and, in the interest of unity, stipulated that the church would not go forward at that time. In the 1995 and 2015 Sessions the issue of ordination per se was not addressed; what was at stake was whether to allow each division to decide for itself in view of its mission.

Second, the matter of ordination is not part of the 28 Fundamental Beliefs of Seventh-day Adventists, nor has it ever been. Unions that have ordained women clergy have not departed from the basic doctrines of the Seventh-day Adventist Church.

Indeed, it can be persuasively argued that these unions in fact are truly complying with the Fundamental Beliefs. This is because No. 14, "Unity in the Body of Christ," contains the following:

In Christ we are a new creation; distinctions of race, culture, learning, and nationality, and differences between high and low, rich and poor, male and female must not be divisive among us.

Third, from the days of the pioneers the church entrusted the question of who might be ordained to the local levels (conference and union conference) rather than to the General Conference. The latter disputes this interpretation of our history, but several Adventist scholars, including historian George Knight, come down on the side of the unions rather than the General Conference. We will return to this point in the next section, where we look at policy.

Fourth, for advocates of women's ordination the issue is one of conscience—recognition of the equality of women and men bestowed by our Creator. As faithful Seventh-day Adventists they are bound before God to obey conscience rather than policy when policy conflicts with conscience.

For this reason, an issue that touches the core of Adventist identity, that is in our DNA, can never be solved by attempting a top-down imposition. Any Adventist worth their salt knows that conscience must trump policy. I am astounded that the leaders in Silver Spring, seat of the Department of Public Affairs and Religious Liberty, and home of the International Religious Liberty Association, could have failed to grasp this essential factor in the dynamic.

But what about those on the other side, whose conscience leads them to oppose ordination of women clergy? Doesn't their conscience also count?

Indeed. The Bible supplies the way out of this dilemma where conscience opposes conscience. Paul has already shown us how to proceed in his letter to the Christians in Rome. From what he writes we find that followers of Jesus there were divided over questions of food. Some felt that because of conscience they could eat only vegetables; others, however, had a clear conscience as carnivores. Paul's counsel? Respect the conscience of every believer in Christ; don't try to impose uniformity of practice. (See Romans 14:1-23.)

The only biblical way forward for Seventh-day Adventists is to permit each division of the world church to decide what is best for the church where it is on the ground.

Fifth, the circumstances of the Adventist church in China make a mockery of the official attempt to prevent women's ordination elsewhere. Adventists have a large and growing church in China, and it is served by thousands of women ministers. Upon completion of their training at the state-run seminary, they are ordained.

If ordination of women is so out of line as to call for drastic action against the Pacific and Columbia Union conferences, how can the General Conference remain silent in view of this situation? To argue that the special circumstances prevailing in China require accommodation to the state is patently unsatisfactory. If women's ordination were a departure from something fundamental to Seventh-day Adventist beliefs and practices, our believers there should be called to oppose it, taking a stand just as they would if, say, the state required them to change their day of worship from the Sabbath to Sunday.

Sixth, the manner in which the San Antonio Session handled the women's ordination issue leaves in doubt the accuracy of the vote. I am greatly troubled by two aspects at San Antonio: the failure to highlight the role of women ministers in China, and the failure to bring before the Session a report of the commission specifically established to investigate the issue. The commission, international in composition, met several times for lengthy discussions. Hundreds of thousands of dollars must have been expended on travel and accommodation for its members. It reached the same conclusion as the commission of the 1970s—no consensus was possible because neither the Bible nor the writings of Ellen White speak directly to the issue. Therefore the church needs to accommodate both positions.

Why was this information not shared with the San Antonio Session? On the face of it, it looks like an attempt to suppress the vote favoring women's ordination.

The actual voting process left much to be desired. An electronic system was put in place, again at considerable expense, to ensure that balloting would be kept confidential. When those who developed the system tested it, it worked fine; however, arguments about accuracy arose, and the system installed was never used.

Even more troubling are the allegations of delegates being pressured to vote on the "No" side. Some of these reports came to me, but I tended to discount them. However, in a paper on the role of union conferences written several months before the 2016 Annual Council, respected historian George Knight noted:

> It is widely reported that delegates in at least two divisions on two continents were told in no uncertain terms how to vote on such issues as women's ordination, knowing that they could face a grilling if the secret vote went wrong ("The Role of Union Conferences in Relation to Higher Authorities," p. 15).

In view of this background, I cannot accept that the vote in San Antonio settled the issue of the ordination of women.

Finally, any attempt by General Conference leaders to take over the Pacific or Columbia Unions is certain to fail. The people elected these leaders; the people approved their plans to ordain women. I am not closely acquainted with the church in Norway and other unions favoring women in ministry, but it would surprise me if the people there did not respond negatively with equal passion.

Whatever were the leaders in the General Conference thinking to come up with the "nuclear option"? Do they have their ear to the ground to listen to the people, not just those who support such drastic action?

Even if by some stratagem the nuclear option succeeded, think of the fall-out. A split would inevitably occur: one part of the church acquiescing to the dictates of the General Conference, the other part refusing to comply. The impact on the General Conference Treasury would be disastrous; the entire world church financial structure would be imperiled.

What was driving our leaders? Were they driven by a compulsion to purify the church at whatever cost? Were they obsessed with preserving the authority of the General Conference? I have no idea; I am baffled.

We turn now to the relation of union conferences to the General Conference.

The Role of Union Conferences

There is a delicious irony in the General Conference's current efforts to bring the non-compliant unions into line. It is this: a major reason for establishing union conferences was to provide a check on excessive exercise of power by the General Conference! Now the shoe is on the other foot.

For the first 40 or 50 years of our existence, Adventists had only two levels of structure—conferences and the General Conference. As the movement grew and expanded to areas beyond North America, problems of administration became increasingly more acute.

The General Conference in Battle Creek, consisting of only a small group of men, micromanaged the work in all its growing totality. This meant that leaders in local conferences had to wait weeks or months to get a decision from headquarters. It was an untenable arrangement.

At the same time, those controlling the whole church from the cockpit in Battle Creek grew more and more autocratic; they arrogated power to themselves. Ellen White didn't approve of what was going on. From her "exile" in Australia she penned increasingly critical messages that protested the "kingly power" exercised at the General Conference. She was not one to mince words: she called for the removal from leadership of those who had become power-drunk.

Out of this background union conferences came into being. The first one was developed in the Australasian field where A. G. Daniells was president and Ellen White was in residence. An experiment, it was strongly opposed by some leaders; however, it soon showed its advantages as important decisions could be taken without delay by people on the ground.

Returning to America in 1900. Ellen White called the church to major reorganization: The autocratic role of the General Conference was to be broken by establishing a new, intermediary link between conferences and the General Conference—the union conferences. And leaders at all levels, especially at the General Conference, were to guide the church humbly without attempting to exercise high-handed authority.

After many meetings, the General Conference Session of 1901 implemented these changes. Ellen White was delighted. So determined were those at the Session to reverse course on kingly power that the new leader of the General Conference, A. G. Daniells, was now designated as "chairman" rather than as president (an arrangement that lasted only two years, after which the church reverted to the presidential structure).

In today's church, leaders from the General Conference side and the union conference side are in agreement as to the origin and purposes of the introduction of union conferences. But what about the responsibilities of each, specifically vis-à-vis questions of ordination? Here the interpretations of history and policy diverge. Union conference leaders can point to categorical statements of policy that specified the lower levels of the church (initially conferences, later union conferences) as being responsible for issues of ordination, including who may or may not be ordained. The General Conference puts a different spin on these policies, arguing that it is there, not the union conferences, where questions of ordination are to be adjudicated.

Several Adventist scholars, notably Gary Patterson ("Does the General Conference Have Authority?") and the late Gerry Chudleigh ("Who Runs the Church? Understanding the Unity, Structure and Authority of the Seventh-day Adventist Church," 2013), have written carefully researched papers that came down on the side of the unions. The General Conference has vigorously opposed the reasoning and conclusion of these studies. Recently, however, respected historian George R. Knight has released his own study of the history and policies ("The Role of Union Conferences in Relation to Higher Authority"). He concludes that the data point to Patterson and Chudleigh as stating the position correctly.

At the very least, we can conclude that the General Conference's defense of its authority to bring unions into line is not as strong as has been claimed, and in fact may be suspect.

The Reaction of the Norwegian Union

The plans developed by the General Conference have created a firestorm. Deeply concerned leaders and laypeople from several countries have expressed alarm and urged cautious reconsideration before any attempt to discipline non-compliant unions. In the Norwegian Union, leaders prepared a classic response, which warrants careful, prayerful consideration by Adventists everywhere. I reproduce it in its entirety.

"The document *A Study of Church Governance and Unity* published recently by the General Conference Secretariat seeks, it claims, to develop unity in the Seventh-day Adventist Church. The document has a number of weaknesses and is likely to contribute to the splitting of the church over the issue of equality for women in ministry. An attempt to coerce unions to comply with General Conference Working Policy is likely to set in motion a series of uncontrollable and unpredictable events.

Oversimplification

"A major weakness of the lengthy document from the Secretariat is over simplification of the issue under consideration: the Adventist church's approach to the ordination of women. The basic assumption on which the argument of the document is based is this: Unity can only be achieved by getting deviant unions in line with General Conference Working Policy.

"It is understandable that the General Conference Secretariat, whose function is to ensure that Seventh-day Adventist entities follow the General Conference Working Policy, writes only in terms of policy compliance, but it is a dangerous oversimplification based on pragmatic rather than moral and spiritual considerations.

"Those unions which have ordained female pastors or stopped ordaining altogether do so because they are convinced that the Bible tells them to treat men and women equally. Their decisions are not grounded in policy but in spiritual and moral obligation.

"The document does not properly take into account the theological understanding that has motivated unions to a course of action different to the stipulations of the Working Policy. This failure in understanding means that the document will not actually provide a basis for stronger unity but rather the contrary.

"The work of the Theology of Ordination Study Committee (TOSC) ended by presenting two opposite understandings of the biblical material on the ordination of women. When a worldwide church study of ordination concluded that both views are legitimate, it is futile now to call upon Working Policy to deny that diversity.

Diversity

"Section III of the document discusses 'Diversity, Union, and Authority' and states: 'In the Bible, diversity is a positive quality, not a negative one.' (p. 10). The same is true in the writings of Ellen G. White. The document goes on to raise the question of how the limits to diversity are to be defined. The Secretariat proposes the principle that decisions on the limits of diversity should be defined 'collectively and collaboratively, not unilaterally.' (p. 12).

"The document considers the early church council in Jerusalem (Acts 15), saying it 'is significant almost as much for its process as for the theological decision that resulted.' (p. 13). The document ignores the fact that there are two major factors for the success of the decision at the Jerusalem council. One factor was how the Holy Spirit led to positions they previously held unthinkable as well as working mightily among gentiles. In the council, Peter told how he was asked to visit Cornelius, and Paul and Barnabas witnessed concerning their work among gentiles. The second major factor was the apostles' brave leadership of guiding the church into a totally new understanding of Scripture, making room for different practices in the church.

"In the Old Testament, God had prescribed a manner of worship, and from their plain reading of the Scriptures, the Jews had drawn the conclusion that 'it was improbable that He would ever authorize a change in any of its specifications.' (AA 189). Still, the leadership of the church helped members to a broadened view. Ellen G. White says, 'the very existence of the Church' depended on this decision (AA 192).

"At the General Conference Session in San Antonio in 2015, the Seventh-day Adventist Church decided to deny the principle that guided the Jerusalem Council and made it a success. The work of the Holy Spirit through female pastors in China was not mentioned. Delegates decided against diversity in the practice of ordination. Previously, in the years while TOSC did its work, the General Conference leadership had followed a strategy of conspicuous silence regarding how to handle diversity. The General Conference behaved very differently from the apostles at the Jerusalem council, providing no leadership to the church on a very divisive issue. We believe that the General Conference leadership must take responsibility for its failure to reach a decision that would create the possibility for different practices to exist harmoniously, side by side within the church. Because of the 'no-vote' in San Antonio, we are now in a much more difficult situation than we were in prior to San Antonio.

Need for leadership to lead

"The question of ordination of female ministers has undoubtedly been the most divisive and most difficult issue the Seventh-day Adventist Church has faced in recent decades. When facing divisive issues, the church needs competent leadership. However, the General Conference President has made no attempt to create space for divisions and unions to allow ordination of women. The TOSC had not ruled any of the presented views as illegitimate. Therefore, there was an obligation for the General Conference leadership to set aside divisive personal convictions and work for a unifying solution.

"The General Conference was repeatedly urged to give a recommendation to the delegates to the San Antonio session. Most notably many members of the General Conference Executive Committee pleaded with leadership at the 2014 Annual Council to give guidance to the delegates. Leadership declined. The failure to create space for different views on the ordination of women to ministry was a grave mistake.

"Elder Wilson made clear his personal opposition to the ordination of women, but he never attempted to defuse the situation by calling for a solution that would accommodate both sides. If unity was high on the agenda of the General Conference leaders prior to San Antonio, they did not use the most obvious opportunity to create it.

"The study document released by the General Conference Secretariat says not one word about the obligation of the General Conference leadership to safeguard unity by creating space for different practices. That is a major weakness of the document.

Dialogue is better than confrontation

"Joshua 22 recounts a story showing the value of dialogue in changing policy. After the conquest of Israel, the account in Joshua 22 describes how some tribes heard that the two and a half tribes that took land on the other side of the Jordan had erected an altar. The Israelites assembled for war against the two and a half tribes. They would not tolerate a departure from policy.

"However, after representatives had talked with the leaders of the two and a half tribes, the situation was defused. War was avoided. The unauthorized altar was accepted.

"Ellen G. White comments on the issue: 'How often serious difficulties arise from a simple misunderstanding, even among those who are actuated by the worthiest motives; and without the exercise of courtesy and forbearance, what serious and even fatal results may follow' (PP 519).

"She continues to draw lessons of the greatest importance and relevance for the Seventh-day Adventist Church in the present crisis: 'While very sensitive to the least blame in regard to their own course, many are too severe in dealing with those whom they suppose to be in error. No one was ever reclaimed from a wrong position by censure and reproach; but many are thus driven further from the right path and led to harden their hearts against conviction. A spirit of kindness, a courteous, forbearing deportment may save the erring and hide a multitude of sins. The wisdom displayed by the Reubenites and their companions is worthy of imitation.... Those who are actuated by the spirit of Christ will possess that charity which suffers long and is kind' (PP 519-520).

"This is the kind of attitude needed to make sure the Seventh-day Adventist Church stays united. Only actions bearing the qualities of the fruit of the spirit will bring true unity among the people of God. 'But the fruit of the Spirit is love, joy, peace, patience, kindness, goodness, faithfulness, gentleness, self-control; against such things there is no law' (Gal 5:22.23).

Assessment of possible outcomes

"It has become known that the General Conference is working on a document outlining how to discipline unions that do not comply with policy. Information from the General Conference indicates that the church leadership wants to use considerable pressure to get unions in line with the Working Policy. It is our experience that few of the documents presented by the General Conference to the Executive Committee contain any assessment of possible outcome scenarios. Therefore, it is important to ask, what are the implications of the church leadership's failure to consider possible responses to the propositions in the present document?

"We have noted above that the document 'A Study of Church Governance and Unity' is oversimplifying the issue. Any thinking along the lines that an Executive Committee action would coerce unions into line is far too optimistic. The major problem with this thinking is that the General Conference is appealing to policy, but for the unions in question this is a question of a biblical and moral mandate.

"In a showdown along these lines, the General Conference is bound to lose. We are Seventh-day Adventists. We know by heart Acts 5:29: 'We ought to obey God rather than men.'

"Here are some possible outcomes that must be considered:

1. "Unions accept the urge to return to following the General Conference Working Policy. This is probably what the General Conference is intending. It is, however, an unlikely outcome, given the biblical, moral, and, in some cases, legal obligations felt by some unions that they have to treat men and women equally.

2. "The General Conference tries to replace union leadership in unions that do not comply with the Working Policy. Any such move will most certainly meet with strong opposition and may turn out to be impossible to accomplish because the actions of these unions are an expression of the convictions of the members in those unions.

3. "General Conference will lose further credibility among large segments of the membership because of the handling of the situation.

4. "The Church will split. The affected unions may sever connections with the Seventh-day Adventist Church. A domino effect may take place where many other unions leave the Seventh-day Adventist Church. By trying to coerce unions, a series of uncontrollable and unforeseen events will develop.

"The probability of splitting the church by voting harsh measures against unions which do not fully comply with the General Conference Working Policy is arguably higher than the probability of achieving the desired outcome of unity. That must be a sobering thought for everyone involved, particularly for the members of the General Conference Executive Committee.

There is always more than one option

"The document *A Study of Church Governance and Unity* released by the General Conference Secretariat leaves the impression that the compliance of the Unions is the only solution to current problems.

"However, in any situation, there are always several options. Discerning leaders will always try to present various options when facing an issue that is a violation neither of any of the Fundamental Beliefs nor of any clear biblical principle. To think there is only one option available is very dangerous for an Executive Committee facing crisis.

"Here are some possible options that may better preserve unity:

1. "Leave the situation as it is. Continue a genuine dialogue with all parties in order to find workable solutions.
2. "Work constructively toward a healing solution along the lines of Acts 15, opening up for diversity. It is within the power of the General Conference Executive to vote changes to the General Conference Working Policy that will ensure unity in diversity.
3. "Create a new gender-inclusive credential. It is the prerogative of the General Conference Executive Committee to create new policies.
4. "Discontinue ordination in its present form. Specify a simple prayer of dedication as the norm when people begin ministry in the Seventh-day Adventist Church.
5. "Table the proposal and give further study to finding means of healing.

"Never before in the history of the Seventh-day Adventist Church have we been closer to a major split of the church. May leaders and members of the Executive Committee take to heart the lessons from Joshua 22 and Acts 15 and make wise decisions that will truly foster unity in our Church, despite our differences."

Conclusion: Top Down or Bottom Up?

For the Roman Catholic Church, unity flows down from the top. It is an imposed unity, more like uniformity.

Historically for Seventh-day Adventists, unity flows from the bottom up. The center of our church is not in Silver Spring, Maryland, but in each local congregation around the world.

Our unity comes not from policies made by humans but from the Holy Spirit. "I in them, and You in Me; that they may be made perfect in one, and that the world may know that You have sent Me, and have loved them as You have loved Me," said Jesus (John 17:23, NKJV). "Make every effort to keep the unity of the Spirit through the bond of peace," admonished the Apostle Paul (Ephesians 4:3, NIV). Here, in the local congregation where we gather to sing, pray, worship, study the Word, and go forth energized to tell others about Jesus—here is where unity happens. This unity flows out to the local conference, the union conference, the General Conference.

"The real question facing the denomination is How catholic do we really want to be?" says George Knight in his recent study. He concludes his hard-hitting paper with "After 115 years Adventism is still faced with the Romish temptations of kingly power and top-down authority."

In 2013 the Southeastern California Conference elected a new president by an overwhelming margin at a duly called constituency meeting. Under the new leadership the conference has grown and prospered financially. Yet when this president appears at an Annual Council, no official badge is waiting, nor the voice and vote accorded other conference presidents. The official Yearbook of the Seventh-day Adventist Church lists all the other presidents around the world, but for the Southeastern California Conference it leaves a blank line.

Dr. Sandra Roberts, elected by the people of her conference, is a woman. The General Conference refuses to acknowledge her—it's as though she does not exist.

Top down or bottom up?

Made in the USA
San Bernardino, CA
21 December 2017